Religions and Religious Movements

CHRISTIANITY

Other books in the Religions and
Religious Movements series:

Buddhism
Confucianism
Hinduism
Islam
Judaism

Religions and Religious Movements

CHRISTIANITY

Gary Zacharias, Book Editor

Bruce Glassman, Vice President

Bonnie Szumski, Publisher, Series Editor

Helen Cothran, Managing Editor

GREENHAVEN PRESS
An imprint of Thomson Gale, a part of The Thomson Corporation

THOMSON

GALE

Detroit • New York • San Francisco • San Diego • New Haven, Conn.
Waterville, Maine • London • Munich

LIBRARY OF CONGRESS CATALOGING-IN-PUBLICATION DATA

Christianity / Gary Zacharias, book editor.
    p. cm. — (Religions and religious movements)
Includes bibliographical references and index.
ISBN 0-7377-2565-6 (lib. : alk. paper)
    1. Christianity. I. Zacharias, Gary. II. Series.
BR121.3.C47 2006
270—dc22   2005040228

Printed in the United States of America

Contents

Chapter 4: Christianity: Its Legacy and Its Future

Foreword

"Religion is not what is grasped by the brain, but a heart grasp."
—Mohandas Gandhi, 1956

The impulse toward religion—to move beyond the world as we know it and ponder the larger questions of why we are here, whether there is a God who directs our lives, and how we should live—seems as universally human as breathing.

Yet, although this impulse is universal, different religions and their adherents are often at odds due to conflicts that stem from their opposing belief systems. These conflicts can also occur because many people have only the most tentative understanding of religions other than their own. In a time when religion seems to be at the root of growing tensions around the world, its study seems particularly relevant.

We live in a religiously diverse world. And while the world's many religions have coexisted for millennia, only recently, with information shared so easily and travel to even the most remote regions made possible for larger numbers of people, has this fact been fully acknowledged. It is no longer possible to ignore other religions, regardless of whether one views these religions positively or negatively.

The study of religion has also changed a great deal in recent times. Just a few decades ago in the United States, few students were exposed to any religion other than Christianity. Today, the study of religion reflects the pluralism of American society and the world at large. Religion courses and even current events classes focus on non-Christian religions as well as the religious experiences of groups that have in the past been marginalized by traditional Christianity, such as women and racial minorities.

In fact, the study of religion has been integrated into many different types of classes and disciplines. Anthropology, psychology, sociology, history, philosophy, political science, economics, and other fields often include discussions about different nations' religions and beliefs.

The study of religion involves so many disciplines because, for many cultures, it is integrated into many different parts of life. This point is often highlighted when American companies conduct business deals in Middle Eastern countries and inadvertently offend a host country's religious constrictions, for example. On both a small scale, such as personal travel, and on a large scale, such as international trade and politics, an understanding of the world's religions has become essential.

The goals of the Religions and Religious Movements series are several. The first is to provide students a historical context for each of the world's religions. Each book focuses on one religion and explores, through primary and secondary sources, its fundamental belief system, religious works of importance, and prominent figures. By using articles from a variety of sources, each book provides students with different theological and historical contexts for the religion.

The second goal of the series is to explore the challenges that each religion faces today. All of these religions are experiencing challenges and changes—some theological, some political—that are forcing alterations in attitude and belief. By reading about these current dilemmas, students will come to understand that religions are not abstract concepts, but a vital part of peoples' lives.

The last and perhaps most important objective is to make students aware of the wide variety of religious beliefs, as well as the factors, common to all religions. Every religion attempts to puzzle out essential questions as well as provide a model for doing good in the world. By using the books in the Religions and Religious Movements series, students will find that people with divergent, closely held beliefs may learn to live together and work toward the same goals.

Introduction

Christianity began as an obscure religious sect in a distant corner of the Roman Empire and developed into the most powerful organization in the world. It remains the largest world religion, with an estimated 2 billion adherents around the globe. For nearly two thousand years it has profoundly influenced the form and development of Western civilization. One area in particular is worth noting: Christianity's role in fostering education.

In light of Christianity's roots in Judaism, an emphasis on education beyond simply spreading Christianity's religious message is not surprising. Judaism has particularly strong traditions of instruction, and the Jewish synagogue has always served as both a place of worship and a center of learning and scriptural study for Jewish children and adults alike.

Jesus of Nazareth, the founder of Christianity and himself of Jewish origins, is from the earliest accounts portrayed as a great teacher. The reader encounters Jesus repeatedly, among both friends and enemies, using dialogue, parables, and real-life examples to explain difficult theological concepts about God, the afterlife, the condition of the human soul, sin, and redemption. Christian scholar Lynn Hartley Millar describes the role of Jesus as teacher this way: "Had Christ left this world without making any provision for carrying on his work, he would still have been the greatest teacher of all time, and his life and example would have influenced profoundly the whole development of educational theory."[1]

According to Christian scripture, shortly before he ascended to heaven the resurrected Jesus Christ told his disciples to model his behavior by educating others. Accordingly, the Twelve Apostles carried on his practice of informal teaching. The historian Luke notes continual religious training, while Paul, the hugely influential missionary, in his letters repeatedly makes reference to Christians teaching in various cities he has visited—Ephesus, Rome, Corinth, Thessalonica. When he lists the qualifications of a bishop (spiritual leader), Paul says such a person has to be able to teach.

Establishing the Earliest Church Schools

After the first generation of disciples, the early church began to establish a more formal program of educating followers, and written treatises on doctrine and practices began to appear. One important early Christian document, the Didache, was essentially a handbook for those who had recently converted to Christianity. Written by unknown authors sometime between A.D. 80 and 110, it combined moral, liturgical, and disciplinary instruction, and shows that education was basic to the life of early Christian communities.

Early in the second century A.D., the Christian bishop Ignatius emphasized that Christian children should be taught the scriptures much like Jewish children were taught Jewish scriptures. Adults too undertook a period of study lasting several years, largely presented in oral question-and-answer form, to prepare for church membership. This instructional method led to formal schools, some of which were established by Justin Martyr, often called the first great scholar of the Christian Church, about 150.

These schools taught more than Christian doctrine; their curricula was known to include mathematics, medicine, and grammar. Historian William Boyd notes that these schools had far-reaching effects on Roman society at large: "Through them, Christianity became for the first time a definite factor in the culture of the world."[2] Modern students may find it especially interesting that these early Christian schools appear to have been the first in which both sexes were taught in the same setting. They took as their model Jesus, who spent a great deal of his time teaching women along with men. According to many historians, Romans did not formally educate girls; Christians, in contrast, educated both girls and women. The early Christian schools further departed from common practice in Greek and Roman societies by taking a universal approach—students were accepted from all social classes and ethnic backgrounds.

Preserving Christian Texts During the Middle Ages

After the fall of the Roman Empire in 476, Christian priests and monks, working in so-called scriptoriums, painstakingly hand-copied ancient Greco-Roman texts, preserving them for future generations. Meanwhile, in reaction to a resurgence of paganism amid the disintegration of centuries-old institutions, Christian hermits sought solitary relationships with God in the deserts of Egypt and Syria. Benedict of Nursia started his Christian life as a hermit. He gained a reputation as a holy man, attracted followers, and found it necessary to establish some sort of community for the practice of the faith in line with a growing monastic movement in Europe. Benedict founded a monastery at Monte Cassino, Italy, in 528 and went on to start twelve other monasteries in other locations.

The Benedictine order and others like it in the monastic movement placed a high value on preserving the literary treasures of antiquity and of Christianity. According to popular historian Daniel Boorstin, for his encouragement of books and learning Benedict deserves to be called "the godfather of libraries."[3] The members of the monasteries set up elaborate library systems, collected books, copied manuscripts, and lent books to other monasteries. Furthermore, monastic rules required monks to read books daily.

While monks in monasteries worked on preserving texts, other Christians attempted to spread literacy be-

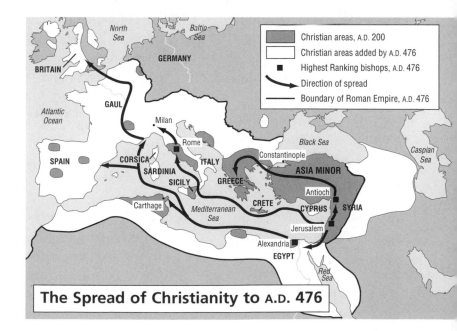

The Spread of Christianity to A.D. 476

yond monastery walls. For example, the Christian bishop Ulfilas, who lived in the mid-300s, introduced Christianity to Germanic barbarian tribes. After ten years of missionary work, he conceived of the idea of translating the Bible into the vernacular, or native tongue of the Goths. To do so, he had to create a new alphabet, using his knowledge of Greek and Latin. He succeeded in translating all books of the Bible except 1 and 2 Kings, which he felt would wrongly encourage the warlike impulses of the Germanic tribes. Ulfilas's translation was important, as historian Kenneth Scott Latourette notes, because it was "probably the first or second instance of what has since happened for hundreds of tongues—their reduction to writing by Christian missionaries and the translation into them by that medium of a part or all of the Scriptures."[4]

Another example of such teaching is that of Cyril and Methodius, ninth-century Greek brothers and fellow monks who were asked by a group of Slavic people to work as missionaries in their region of eastern Europe. In preparation for their task, Cyril invented an alphabet to write Slavic languages; the modern-day Cyrillic alphabet of Russia and Central Asia is named for him, though there is some dispute over whether that is actually the alphabet of Cyril.

Developing the Liberal Arts

Medieval Christianity also fostered the development of the so-called liberal arts, which would form the core curriculum of the universities of Europe for centuries. To produce an educated clergy capable of administering church affairs, medieval monastery and church schools, also called cathedral schools and usually staffed by clerics, offered instruction beyond theology and Latin. These schools incorporated two additional groups of subjects, codified in antiquity as the trivium (in Latin, "three roads") and quadrivium ("four roads"). The trivium comprised lessons in grammar, rhetoric, and logic. The subjects of the quadrivium were arithmetic, geometry, astronomy, and harmonics (music). Together, these seven subjects were known as the seven liberal arts, which the church advanced as the foundation of higher learning.

Beginning in the late eleventh century, these educational centers gradually evolved into communities of scholars promoted by the church, with organized courses of study, a faculty who had completed the curricula themselves and who could confer degrees, and a student body of would-be scholars who were expected to interpret sacred texts and prove their mastery of the curricula through oral examination. The university was born, first in Bologna and by the early thirteenth century in Paris, Oxford, Cambridge, and Naples. New York University historian Joseph Reither notes that "universities were the creation of the Middle Ages."[5]

The universities of Bologna, Paris, and Oxford originally offered study in theology, Aristotelian physics and physiology, and church and civil law. Their methods were as important as their subject matter: Instruction was presented in a systematic, thorough way and tested by rigorous philosophical debate and examination, setting standards upheld by universities to the present day.

One of the major innovations of the early universities was an emphasis on what would today be called empirical research, meaning knowledge derived from direct observation or experimentation as opposed to pure reasoning. For example, students at the University of Bologna dissected human cadavers for forensic purposes to settle legal suits. Reasoning, particularly the formal kind of question-and-answer reasoning known as dialectic, was still of highest importance, and medieval scholars applied reasoning to arrive at all kinds of knowledge, including spiritual truths and defenses of Christian dogma. The great English mathematician and philosopher Alfred North Whitehead states, "The Middle Ages formed one long training of the intellect of Western Europe in the sense of order. . . . It was pre-eminently an epoch of orderly thought, rationalist through and through."[6]

Increasing Literacy Through the Reformation

The Reformation, a religious movement of the 1500s that gave rise to Protestantism, was responsible for widespread changes in education. Although the early church had allowed the education of all social classes and ethnic backgrounds, broad religious education had deteriorated by the time the German monk Martin Luther attacked corrupt church practices in the early 1500s. In general, Europeans submitted to church authority but knew little of church teachings and could not follow church services, which were conducted in Latin, a language few common people understood.

Luther, displeased by such widespread ignorance, wrote his *Small Catechism* in 1529 to instruct people in basic professions of the faith such as the Lord's Prayer and the Ten Commandments. Luther also translated the Bible from Latin into German in line with his conviction that the Bible alone, not the pope and his tax-collecting clerical emissaries, should be the guide to life and religious belief. Luther also believed that people could communicate with God directly and thus that cultivating the human mind was absolutely essential, according to historian Mark A. Noll, "to understand both the word of scripture and the nature of the world in which the word would take root."[7] Luther urged the establishment of a state school system free to all without regard to social standing. He also suggested students should be compelled to attend school, making him the first modern writer to urge compulsory school attendance.

Another early Protestant reformer played a role in bringing literacy to the masses. Noted educator Samuel L. Blumenfeld writes that the roots of universal education go back to the French theologian John Calvin:

> The modern idea of popular education—that is, education for everyone—first arose in Europe during the Protestant Reformation when papal authority was replaced by biblical authority. Since the Protestant rebellion against Rome had arisen in part as a result of biblical study and interpretation, it became obvious to Protestant leaders that if the reform movement were to survive and flourish, widespread biblical literacy, at all levels of society, would be absolutely necessary.[8]

The importance of John Calvin to modern education cannot be overstated. Everywhere his philosophy spread, throughout northern Europe and eventually to America, his concept of the school was a powerful impetus to popular education. Christian historian Lars Qualben writes that Calvin urged "a system of elementary education in the vernacular for all, including reading, writing, arithmetic, grammar, and religion and the establishment of secondary schools for the purpose of training citizens for civil and ecclesiastical leadership."[9] His academy at Geneva, Switzerland, became a model for many of the early colleges and universities established by the Puritans and their successors in America.

Elementary and Higher Education in the United States

The English colonists of North America were predominantly Protestants, committed to Christian upbringing but equally committed to certain democratic ideals such as education. Pilgrims and Puritans made education a high priority when they arrived in America in the early 1600s. They set minimum educational requirements for children and required Christian communities to hire and pay teachers.

The New England Primer, a basic reader for children of the time, exemplified the connection between religious and secular instruction. The primer incorporated simple psalms and biblical verses; through the primary teaching methods of recitation and drills students absorbed Christian values while they mastered basic reading skills. Historians credit Christian educational programs for achieving high rates of literacy in the young United States.

From 1620, when the Pilgrims landed, until the mid-1800s, almost all education in America was private and Christian. Then, led by pioneers such as Horace Mann, state legislatures began to establish so-called common or normal schools. The rapidly growing public-school movement, hailed as the birthright of all American children, viewed education as the solution to poverty and other social ills and the best way to prepare children for responsible citizenship and republican government.

The methods and curricula of the new school systems, however, were based on traditional church school models. For example, the standard textbook was *McGuffey's Eclectic Reader*, a series of primers written by Presbyterian minister William McGuffey between 1841 and 1885. These strongly moralistic books, the backbone of grammar school education for American children, blended instruction in reading and writing with Christian theology and ethics. They had a profound influence on the literary tastes as well as the religious character of generations of schoolchildren in the United States.

Many of the oldest American colleges and universities also have clear Christian associations: Harvard's first benefactor was Puritan minister John Harvard (though the university was never formally affiliated with any religious denomination); Yale University was founded by a group of Congregationalist ministers; and the Reverend James Blair was instrumental in founding the College of William and Mary, where he served as its first president.

The contributions of Christian believers to modern education are many and varied. For example, a Lutheran layman named Johann Sturm introduced graded levels of education in the mid-1500s. Friedrich Froebel, the son of a Lutheran pastor, originated the kindergarten school to help nurture Christian beliefs in the youngest children. Formal education of the deaf grew out of the strong Christian convictions of Abbé Charles-Michel de l'Epée, Thomas Gallaudet, and Laurent Clerc. Scottish printer and devout Christian Robert Raikes began the first Sunday school in 1780 to reach the neglected poor children in his country. Finally, it was a dedicated Christian named Louis Braille who in 1834 created a system of pin-pricked raised dots to help the blind read.

Christianity is arguably the single greatest influence on the course of Western civilization. One of its most effective tools is education, an institution shaped by the faith and in turn shaping the faith for two thousand years.

Notes

1. Lynn Hartley Millar, *Christian Education in the First Four Centuries*. London: Faith Press, 1946, p. 10.
2. William Boyd, *The History of Western Education*. New York: Barnes & Noble, 1965, p. 84.
3. Daniel Boorstin, *The Discoverers*. New York: Vintage, 1983, p. 491.
4. Kenneth Scott Latourette, *A History of the Expansion of Christianity*. Grand Rapids, MI: Zondervan, 1970, p. 214.
5. Quoted in D. James Kennedy and Jerry Newcombe, *What If Jesus Had Never Been Born?* Nashville: Thomas Nelson, 1994, p. 51.
6. Quoted in Vincent Carroll and David Shiflett, *Christianity on Trial*. San Francisco: Encounter, 2002, p. 72.
7. Mark A. Noll, *The Scandal of the Evangelical Mind*. Grand Rapids, MI: Eerdmans, 1994, p. 37.
8. Samuel L. Blumenfeld, *Is Public Education Necessary?* Boise, ID: Paradigm, 1985, p. 10.
9. Lars Qualben, *A History of the Christian Church*. New York: Thomas Nelson and Sons, 1958, p. 270.

CHAPTER 1

Jesus and the Apostles: Origins of Christianity (4 B.C.–A.D. 100)

Jesus Creates a New Religious Movement

by Robert A. Baker

To understand Christianity, one needs to know the world in which it started as well as the life and teachings of its founder, Jesus. In the following excerpt, church historian Robert A. Baker, explains the culture and politics of the world into which Jesus was born, focusing on Greek, Roman, and Jewish influences. He describes Jesus's ministry and explains the rapid growth of the church within this historical context. Baker, former head of the Department of Church History at Southwestern Seminary, is the author of *Relations Between Northern and Southern Baptists*.

Any thoughtful person will look with real curiosity at the description of the apostle Paul in Acts 21:37–40. Paul had stirred up his customary riot, this time in the Temple at Jerusalem, and was only saved from severe injury at the hands of the Jewish mob by the intervention of the Roman soldiers patrolling the city. As Paul endeavors to speak to the people from the stairs of the prison castle, four aspects of his life are presented in quick succession: (1) He spoke the Greek language and

Robert A. Baker, *A Summary of Christian History*. Nashville: Broadman Press, 1959, pp. 2–12. Copyright © 1959 by Broadman Press. Reproduced by permission.

was a citizen of a city noted for its Greek culture. (2) He was a Roman citizen (notice Acts 22:25–29, along with 21:39). (3) He was a Jew and was fluent in the Hebrew tongue. (4) He was a Christian, bearing testimony of the Master to his own race.

The diverse racial, linguistic, and religious elements reflected here are intelligible only as the background of Paul is understood. Here is the function of church history—to explain *why* and *how*. It is impossible to interpret Paul or any part of Christianity without an understanding of the historical background. For the New Testament period this includes Greek, Roman, and Jewish influences. Customs, parties, traditions, and allusions that are meaningless unless they are explained in historical terms constantly crop up in the New Testament.

Greek Influence on Christianity

The Greek elements in the world into which Christianity came may be traced to the conquest of Palestine (and almost all of the known world) by Alexander the Great in the last half of the fourth century before Christ. This Macedonian soldier scattered into almost every part of the known world the tremendous culture and spirit of the Greeks. After Alexander's death his military generals and their successors ruled Palestine for over a century and a half. Without attempting to relate the remarkable history of Greek life and development, the outstanding contributions of that race to the Christian movement may be summed up under three heads.

First, Greek philosophy, some good and some bad, was scattered everywhere. Strangely enough, God used both the good and the bad to prepare for the coming of Christ. The atheistic and skeptical philosophy of the

Greeks turned many in the Gentile world away from the superstitious worship of false gods and intensified their heart-hunger for the true God. The good Greek philosophy, on the other hand, prepared the world for the coming of Christ by magnifying the worth of the human spirit and by placing high value upon spiritual and moral truth.

In the second place, the Greek language became the common tongue throughout the whole Mediterranean world. Even in Palestine good Jews were forced to learn the Greek language in order to carry on trade in the markets. The fact is of more importance than might appear at first glance. For one thing, the missionaries of Christ could begin their work immediately without waiting to learn a new language. Furthermore, the presence of a common language brought a sense of unity to the various races. Compare the present-day slang expression "he speaks my language," suggesting a basic unity. Finally, the language itself was marvelously adequate. The Greeks had developed a language that made it possible to express clearly and precisely the great truths of the Christian revelation. Greek was the language of most (if not all) of the New Testament.

Third, the Greek spirit made its contribution to the Christian movement. It is difficult to put this spirit into words, but it included an intense love for truth, vision that encompassed large sweep, and initiative that was bold and daring.

Roman Influence on Christianity

The constant protection afforded Paul because he was a Roman citizen suggests the contribution of the Roman Empire to the Christian movement. Historically, Greek rule in Palestine ended about 167 B.C. when the Jewish patriots under Judas Maccabeus defeated the Greeks. In 63 B.C., after Jewish independence of about a century, the soldiers of Rome took possession of Palestine. A glance at the New Testament reveals evidence of Roman rule. It speaks of Roman centurions, Roman guards, Roman jailers, Roman castles, Roman governors. One of the questions which the Pharisees asked Jesus concerned whether a good Jew could serve God under Roman rule. The unpopularity of Matthew, the publican, grew out of the fact that he was collecting taxes for Rome.

Roman rule in the world when Jesus was born was not altogether good nor completely bad in its effect upon Christianity. The strong centralized government of Rome provided a measure of peace and protection. Rome would not permit any sort of violence to take place within the borders of her empire, lest the uproar should serve as a cloak for political revolt. This made it possible for Christian missionaries to move among the various races of the Mediterranean world with a minimum of political friction. Roman citizens like Paul were protected from unjust treatment by local officers. The network of Roman roads and ship routes made travel less hazardous and more convenient. Two hundred years later the language of the Romans would be adopted as the principal medium for religious expression.

On the other hand, the world government of Rome became the great enemy of Christianity before the end of the first century. It will be noted that the Roman mind had little conception of the value of an individual soul, choosing, rather, to exhaust religious devotion in the service of the state. The Roman armies adopted the false gods of every nation whom they conquered, only requiring that in return the subjugated nation accept

Roman gods, including the Roman emperor. When
Christians refused to worship the Roman emperor, severe persecution was inflicted.

Jewish Influence on Christianity

The third racial influence upon the Christian movement was the most significant. The Jewish nation provided the immediate background of Christ and all of
his early disciples. The history of the Jews as related in
the Old Testament is too well known to be repeated in
detail. God chose a family of faith which, under divine
care, developed into a nation. Several factors combined
to bring political division about 975 B.C. The Northern
Kingdom was carried into Assyrian captivity about 722
B.C. The Southern Kingdom stood until about 587 B.C.
when it officially fell to the Babylonians. After about
seventy years, remnants of the Southern Kingdom were
permitted by the Persian empire to return to Palestine.
They remained subject to the Persians until about 334
B.C., when Alexander the Great conquered them. The
Greek period (334–167 B.C.), the century of Jewish independence (167–63 B.C.), and the beginning of Roman
rule (63 B.C.) bring the history of the Jewish people to
the New Testament era.

During this long history the Jewish people were, to
some extent unconsciously, making preparation for the
coming of Christ. They carefully preserved the revelation which God had given them. Through adversity and
captivity two great truths were burned into their souls:
first, that there is only one God for men; and second,
that the relationship of God to men is personal, not national. Before the Babylonian captivity the Jews had often fallen into idolatry and polytheism, but after their

return to Palestine they became zealous teachers of the truth that God is one (monotheism). While residents of Palestine, the Jews had sometimes conceived of God in national terms, but in captivity their isolation from every material reminder of a national deity brought them to realize that the *individual* must commune with God through the spirit. It was worth the experiences of the Babylonian captivity to learn this lesson.

Although some, like Jonah, were reluctant to witness to Gentiles, the entire world became familiar with the beliefs and practices of the Jews. Early in the Greek period a movement known as the Dispersion began. This was the voluntary movement of great numbers of Jews from Palestine to almost every part of the Mediterranean world. Wherever they went the Jews made numerous proselytes to their religion, establishing synagogues for teaching God's revelation, witnessing to the sovereignty of one God, and looking into the heavens for the Messiah. This leaven prepared the world for Christ's coming.

The Jewish institutions and parties that form so much a part of the New Testament story have their background in these historical experiences. The synagogue was developed as a place of teaching and worship during the Babylonian captivity when there was no temple available. The prominent place that it held after the return of the Jews from the exile brought into existence the groups known as scribes and lawyers. Their chief duty at first was to copy Scriptures; because they became experts in what the Scriptures said, their duties were enlarged to include scriptural interpretation and instruction.

Perhaps the contact between the Jews and the Persian religious ideas helped to produce the party known as the Essenes, which probably arose about 150 B.C. This group numbered about four thousand at the time of Christ and was characterized by rigorous orthodoxy, celibacy, communal ownership, and the elimination of animal sacrifices in worship. The Pharisees doubtless grew out of the separatist tendency when the overtures of the Samaritans were rejected during the days of Ezra and Nehemiah (about 500 B.C.). During the Maccabean struggle (beginning about 167 B.C.), this party took distinct form. In the New Testament they are pictured as narrow, bigoted, and to some extent hypocritical. They were numerous and popular in the time of Jesus, rallying to traditional supernaturalism and ceremonial exactness. The Sadducees probably arose during the second century before Christ. Friendly to Roman and Greek culture, they represented religious and political liberalism. Their rationalism led them to deny the resurrection and divine providence, to refuse all tradition, and to magnify the freedom of the human will.

The Samaritans arose through the intermarriage of Jews who had been left in Palestine after the beginning of the Babylonian captivity with Gentiles who had been brought into the land. The Herodians were the Jewish political patriots who supported the Herod family against Rome. The Zealots were probably the heirs of the Maccabean tradition of fervent zeal to throw off the yoke of foreigners.

Jesus Christ (4 B.C.–A.D. 30)

Into this sort of world Jesus Christ was born. Practically all that is known of his earthly life may be found in the Synoptic Gospels (Matthew, Mark, and Luke) and in John. John's Gospel describes Jesus' eternal nature and preincarnate existence; Matthew and Luke record his human genealogy. It is likely that Matthew gives the genealogy of Joseph while Luke deals with the genealogy of Mary. Matthew and Luke alone recount the birth and childhood of Jesus and of John the Baptist, the forerunner of Jesus. All of the Gospels speak of John's ministry and look from different points of view at the life of Christ.

The birth of Jesus Christ occurred about 4 B.C. This means that Christ actually began his public ministry about A.D. 27 and was crucified about A.D. 30. The Lord's ministry may be conveniently divided into seven sections. (1) His early Judean ministry, described principally in John's Gospel, includes the calling of the first disciples and the first cleansing of the Temple. (2) The great Galilean ministry covers the principal period of Christ's work and lasted about a year and a half. During this time the Lord was rejected at Nazareth, moved to Capernaum, chose the twelve apostles, set forth the Sermon on the Mount, and toured Galilee three times. (3) His several withdrawals from the press of the crowds gave opportunity for special instruction to the disciples, for securing the great confession at Caesarea Philippi, and for the transfiguration experience. (4) His later Judean ministry continued for about three months and is described by Luke and John. It centered on the attendance of Jesus and his disciples at the Feasts of Tabernacles and Dedication in Jerusalem. (5) His brief Perean ministry is spoken of by all four of the Gospels and is characterized by final miracles, parables, and prophecies of his resurrection. (6) The last week in Jerusalem is treated in great detail by John's Gospel. It begins with the triumphal entry and closes with the crucifixion. (7) The postresurrection ministry of Jesus for about forty days before his ascension marks the close of the Gospel accounts.

The teachings of Jesus are remarkable both in their method and content. He drove home truth through parables, questions, discourses, and debates. God's person and purpose were revealed in Christ's life and teachings. Love is to be the dominant theme of the Christian's life. Because God loved men, Christ died on the cross for man's sins; by personal trust in Christ, men could receive a birth from above and assurance of eternal life. The conquering power of the cross and the ultimate triumph of the kingdom of God were central in Christ's teachings. He established his church, a local autonomous body where two or three gathering together in prayer could find his presence and power.

After the death and ascension of Christ, the disciples whom he had chosen and instructed set out on the seemingly impossible task contained in the Great Commission. Despite efforts of many other religions to attract men, Christianity began growing like a mustard seed. From a human standpoint, many reasons may be advanced for this tremendous development. (1) Heathenism was bankrupt and could not answer the call of hungry hearts. (2) The great welter of religions of every description clamoring for devotees could not compete with God's revelation in Christ. (3) Every Christian became a missionary; the sacred fire leaped from friend to friend. (4) The Christians had a burning conviction that Christ alone could save the lost world about them and that since the return of Christ was imminent, there was no time to be lost.

The seventy years of Christian growth from Christ's death to that of the last apostle may be divided into three periods.

Period of Local Witnessing (A.D. 30–45)

The first twelve chapters of Acts describe the history of the Christian movement during the first fifteen years after Christ's death and resurrection. The Holy Spirit was given in accordance with the promise of Christ, providing power for witnessing in a hostile world, bringing the presence of Christ for fellowship and strength, and giving leadership from Christ in the initiation of important movements. At Pentecost men from every part of the world were saved and doubtless went back to their own cities to establish Christian churches. Persecution, want, and internal bickering were only temporary hurdles (see Acts 3–6).

The martyrdom of Stephen marks a turning point in two respects: it began the persecution that drove the Christians out of Jerusalem into all Judea and Samaria in their witness; and it profoundly moved Saul the persecutor in the direction of personal conversion to Christ. The local witness was expanded by the preaching of Peter to a Gentile (for which he was required to give explanation to the church at Jerusalem), the founding of the Gentile church at Antioch, and the martyrdom of James, son of Zebedee. The conversion of Saul, his preparation for service, and his ministry at Antioch provide the background for the second stage of Christian development.

Period of Missionary Expansion (A.D. 45–68)

Under the leadership of the Holy Spirit a new direction of witnessing was begun with the inauguration of the missionary tours of Paul and Barnabas. Paul is the central figure in at least three great missionary tours between the years 45 and 58, when he was seized in the

Temple at Jerusalem. During these thirteen years he wrote two letters to the church at Thessalonica, two to the Corinthians, one to the Galatians, and one to the Romans. After his imprisonment in Rome about A.D. 61 he wrote the letters known as Philemon, Colossians, Ephesians, and Philippians. He probably was released for four or five years, but the extent of his travel during this time is not known. His two letters known as 1 Timothy and Titus were prepared in this interim. Tradition suggests that he may have gone as far west as Spain on one journey. He was imprisoned again about 67 at Rome. Just before his death at the hands of Nero he wrote 2 Timothy.

It is quite possible that tradition is correct in speaking of extensive missionary activity by other apostles, but such accounts are too meager and too far removed from the occasion to be of much value. It is known that Paul's missionary activity accounts for the rise of practically all of the important Christian centers of the first century. Churches were established through his efforts in some of the strongest cities of the empire.

Between the first and second missionary journeys, Paul and Silas attended a conference at Jerusalem (about 50). James presided at the meeting, and several discussed the question of whether a man needs to become a Jew first in order to become a Christian. After some, including the apostle Peter, had spoken, James gave his decision that any Gentile could find salvation by simple faith in Christ without going through Judaism.

During this period, which closes with the death of the apostle Paul at Rome in A.D. 68, nine other books that form the New Testament were written. These were James, Mark, Matthew, Luke, Acts, 1 Peter, Jude, 2 Peter, and Hebrews, perhaps in that order.

Period of Westward Growth (A.D 68–100)

After Paul's death the center of Christian strength moved toward the western section of the Mediterranean area. Although the material for this period is scarce, it is not difficult to find reasons to substantiate the tradition of the westward move. About the year 66 the Jewish War broke out in Palestine, resulting in the complete destruction of Jerusalem in 70 at the hands of the Roman Titus. This catastrophe marked the end of Herod's Temple and the sacrifices of the Jews; at the same time it uprooted the Christian church in Jerusalem and scattered the people abroad. In which direction should Christianity move? Tradition reports that the apostle John went to Ephesus about the time Jerusalem was destroyed. This is plausible, since the most logical move would be toward the great church centers in the West established by the apostle Paul. Here and there in later literature are hints that Christians may have gone to every part of the western Mediterranean. The tradition of Christianity in Britain is very early; perhaps one of the soldiers chained to the apostle Paul was won by him to Christ and then transferred to the British garrison, there to witness and organize a Christian church. Possibly a similar situation sent the good news to central Europe, North Africa, and elsewhere to the fringes of the Roman Empire.

Conservative scholars assign five books by the apostle John to this period. Written by a "son of thunder," these books contain warnings against diluting Christianity and minimizing either the humanity or the deity of Christ. The advocates of such heretical views cannot be identified, but their presence is significant in view of the rise of these very doctrinal aberrations in the next century. Apparently John was exiled to the Isle of Patmos from Ephesus during the course of a severe persecution by the Roman Emperor Domitian (81–96). The book of Revelation, defying the effort of the Roman Empire to require Christians to worship the Roman emperor, was written in the closing decade of the apostolic period.

Concluding Summary

The literature that became the New Testament canon had not as yet been brought together into one book. The various churches used the Old Testament, together with such Christian writings as they might possess. The evidence shows that at the close of the century the Christian movement was pure in doctrine and growing in numbers. It is true that there were efforts on every hand to dilute the nature of Christianity, but apostolic leadership helped to maintain a strong internal unity.

The functioning New Testament church showed no signs of developing into an ecclesiastical hierarchy or spiritual despotism. It was a local autonomous body with two officers and two ordinances. The two officers were pastor (sometimes called bishop, presbyter or elder, minister, shepherd) and deacon. These leaders usually worked with their hands for their material needs. There was no artificial distinction between clergy and laity. The pastors had no more authority in offering salvation through Christ than did any other member of their body. Their distinguishing marks were the gifts of leadership given them through the Spirit and their willingness to be used of God. In view of the later pretensions of the Roman pastor or bishop, it should be mentioned that each church was completely independent of external control. There is no indication anywhere in the literature of this period that the apostle Peter ever served as pastor in Rome; nor, for that matter, is there any basis for believing that the church at Rome was founded by any apostle. Doubtless it was organized by men converted at Pentecost.

The two ordinances were baptism and the Lord's Supper. These were simply symbolical memorials. Salvation or spiritual gifts did not come through either one. The transference of spiritual regeneration and spiritual merit to these ordinances is a development that comes through later corruptions. Worship was simple, consisting of the singing of hymns, praying, reading of Scriptures, and exhortations.

Paul Spreads Christianity Throughout the Roman Empire

by Earle Edwin Cairns

In the following excerpt, religious historian Earle Edwin Cairns explores the importance of the apostle Saul, later named Paul, who spread Christianity beyond the world of the Jews. Paul was responsible for taking the Christian message to the Roman world, both in Asia Minor and Europe, through his own journeys and in letters to Christian outposts that shaped the doctrine of the early church. Earle Edwin Cairns was professor of history at Wheaton College in Illinois from 1943 to 1977.

The early Jewish-Christian church seemed slow to apprehend the universal character of Christianity even though Peter had been instrumental in giving the gospel to the first Gentile converts. It was Paul who had by revelation of God the largeness of vision to see the need of the Gentile world and to spend his life carrying the gospel to that world. As no other in the early church, Paul realized the universal character of Christianity and dedicated himself to the propagation of it to the ends of the Roman Empire (Rom. 11:13; 15:16). One might well wonder whether he did not have in his mind the slogan "The Roman Empire for Christ" as he slowly made his way westward with the message of the Cross (Rom. 15:15–16, 18–28; Acts 9:15; 22:21). He did not spare himself in achieving this end, but he did not neglect his own people, the Jews. This is evidenced by his seeking out the Jewish synagogue first in every town he came to and by proclaiming the gospel to the Jews and Gentile proselytes as long as they would listen to him.

Paul's Environment

Paul was conscious of three temporal loyalties during the course of his life. He had as a young man the training accorded only to promising young Jews and had sat at the feet of the great Jewish teacher Gamaliel. Few could boast of having better training than Paul as far as Jewish religious education was concerned and few had profited as thoroughly from their training as had Paul (Phil. 3:4–6). He was also a citizen of Tarsus, the leading city of Cilicia, "no mean city" (Acts 21:39). He was also a freeborn Roman citizen (Acts 22:28) and did not hesitate to make use of the privileges of a Roman citizen when such privileges would help in the carrying out of his mission for Christ (Acts 16:37; 25:11). Judaism was his religious environment prior to his conversion. Tarsus, with its great university and intellectual atmosphere, was the scene of his earlier years; and the Roman Empire was the political milieu in which he lived and did his work. Thus Paul grew up in an urban cosmopolitan culture.

This political environment did not seem to be too promising a one for the proclamation of the gospel. Caesar Augustus had brought about the downfall of the republic, except as a political form, when he set up a dyarchy in 27 B.C., in which he nominally shared control of the state with the senate. Unfortunately, his successors had neither the ability nor the character of Augustus, and they were guilty of misrule. Caligula (37–41) was insane during part of his reign; and Nero (54–68), under whom Paul was martyred and the church endured its first persecution, was a cruel and bloody man who did not hesitate to kill members of his own family. However, Claudius (41–54) was an excellent administrator, and the empire was fairly stable during his reign. It was in his reign that Paul made most of his missionary journeys.

The social and moral situation was much more unpromising than the political. Booty from the empire created a wealthy upper class of new aristocrats who had slaves and wealth to pander to their every legitimate and illegitimate desire. This class was somewhat contemptuous of the new religion and saw in its appeal to the poorer classes a threat to their superior position in society. But even some of this class were won by the preaching of the gospel when Paul was a prisoner in Rome (Phil. 1:13).

Rival Religions and Philosophies

Paul also faced the rivalry of competing systems of religion. The Romans were somewhat eclectic in their religious outlook and were willing to give toleration to any faith that would not prevent its worshipers from taking part in the state system of worship, which combined emperor worship with the old republican state worship and claimed the allegiance of all the people in the empire except the Jews, who were exempt by law from its rites. Christians could not, of course, do this and so they faced the problem of opposition from the state. The more subjective mystery religions of Mithra, Cybele, and Isis claimed the allegiance of many others in the empire. Judaism, as Christianity was distinguished from it as a separate sect, offered increasing opposition.

Roman intellectuals accepted philosophical systems, such as Stoicism, Epicureanism, and Neo-Pythagoreanism, that suggested philosophical contemplation as the way to salvation. Stoicism, with its pantheistic view of God, its conception of natural ethical laws to be discovered by reason, and its doctrine of the fatherhood of God and the brotherhood of man, seemed to provide a philosophical foundation for the Roman Empire. Some of the emperors, such as Marcus Aurelius (161–80), found its ethical standards appealing. It was this confused religious scene that Paul had to face with the simple redemptive gospel of the death of Christ.

Archaeology helps us to date key points in Paul's life and work. Paul had been in Corinth eighteen months when Gallio became proconsul (Acts 18:12–13). An inscription on stone discovered at Delphi mentions that Gallio began his duties in Achaia in the twenty-sixth year of Claudius, which was A.D. 51–52. Thus Paul's visit would have begun eighteen months before, in A.D. 50. Other dates in his life can be calculated from this date with relative accuracy.

Paul's conversion was also an objective historical event. He spoke of it as such in 1 Corinthians 9:1 and 15:8 and in Galatians 1:11–18. This was brought about by his contact with Christ on the road to Damascus (Acts 9; 22; and 26). This experience was vital to his later missionary work, teaching, writings, and theology.

Paul's genius was so many-sided that it is necessary to

give consideration to his work under different categories. Each of the discussions will emphasize the magnitude of the task that God gave him and the devotion with which he worked to accomplish the appointed task.

The Propagator of the Gospel

Paul was a wise as well as devoted missionary, and his life illustrates the use of principles that have served many well in seeking to carry out Christ's great commission to the church. A consideration of the maps of his journeys reveals the advance of the gospel under his preaching along a great semicircle reaching from Antioch to Rome. Paul adopted as a basic principle the expansion of the gospel to the West, and it must have been with delight that he first caught sight of his goal, Rome, even if it was as a prisoner of the Roman government.

Paul also thought in terms of areas that could be reached from strategic urban centers. He always started his work in a new area in the most strategic city and used the converts to carry the message to the surrounding towns and countryside. Because of this practice it is not likely that he visited Colosse (Col. 2:1) but rather that the strong church in that town was founded by those whom he sent from Ephesus.

Paul began his work in strategic Roman centers by going first to the synagogue, where he proclaimed his message as long as he was well received. When opposition arose, he turned to a direct proclamation of the gospel to the Gentiles in any place that he found suitable. His principle was to preach to the Gentile after he had given the message to the Jew. This principle may be seen by a study of accounts of the journeys recorded in Acts (Rom. 1:16).

After founding a church, Paul would organize it with

elders and deacons so that the church might be self-governing after his departure. He sought to build on solid foundations.

Paul's desire not to be a burden to the infant churches led him to assume the responsibility of supporting himself while he preached in a new area. He worked at his trade of tentmaking while he preached to the people in Corinth (Acts 18:1–4; cf. 1 Thess. 2:9). He did not make this a rule for others but felt that it was a necessity for his work. The church was also to be self-supporting.

His dependence on the Holy Spirit's guidance in his work is clearly evident in both the Acts and his epistles (Acts 13:2, 4; 16:6–7). He did not wish to go to any place unless there was clear evidence that it was the field in which God would have him labor. He sought to reach the areas untouched by others so that he might be a pioneer of the gospel (Rom. 15:20). This pioneering spirit was productive in that it resulted in his carrying the gospel from Antioch to Rome and, possibly, as far west as Spain during his lifetime.

These principles that the apostle followed served him well in the development of churches that were organized centers for the continued preaching of the gospel. He did not leave them without supervision, for he made a practice of revisiting or writing letters to the churches that he founded in order to encourage and to strengthen them (Acts 15:36). One does not wonder at the rapid growth of Christianity under such sane yet inspired leadership. The church was self-propagating also.

Paul's Publications

Paul made a practice of keeping in touch with the local situation in each church through visitors from that

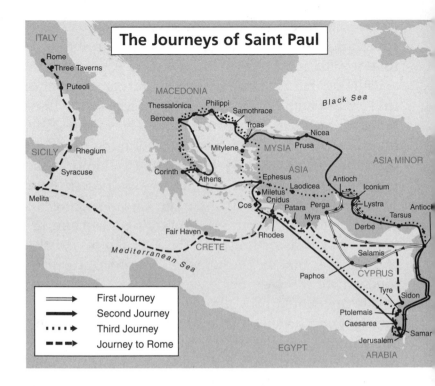

The Journeys of Saint Paul

ITALY
Rome
Three Taverns
Puteoli
MACEDONIA
Thessalonica Philippi
Beroea   Samothrace
Troas
Black Sea
SICILY   Rhegium
Mitylene   MYSIA Prusa
Nicea
Syracuse
Corinth   ASIA
Athens   Ephesus   Antioch   ASIA MINOR
Melita
Miletus   Laodicea   Iconium
Cnidus
Cos   Patara Perga   Lystra   Antioch
Myra   Tarsus
Fair Haven
Derbe
CRETE   Rhodes
Mediterranean Sea
Salamis
Paphos   CYPRUS
Tyre   Sidon
First Journey
Second Journey   Ptolemais
Third Journey   Caesarea
Journey to Rome   Jerusalem   Samar
EGYPT
ARABIA

church (1 Cor. 1:11) or through the reports of agents whom he sent to visit the churches (1 Thess. 3:6). Whenever the local situation seemed to demand it, he wrote letters under the guidance of the Holy Spirit to deal with particular problems. He wrote twice to the Thessalonian church to clear up misunderstandings concerning the doctrine of the second coming of Christ. The Corinthian church faced the problems of a church in a large pagan city, and Paul addressed his first letter to the solution of their problems. Questions concerning human and spiritual wisdom peculiar to a church in a cultured Greek city (1 Cor. 1–4), the problem of morality in a pagan environment (chap. 5), lawsuits between Christians before pagan judges (6), marriage problems (7), and the problem of social relationships with pagan idolaters (8–10) were some of the matters with which Paul had to deal by correspondence. His Second Epistle to the Corinthians grew out of the need to assert his apostleship so that his authority to act as stated in the first letter would be confirmed. The letter to the Galatians was made necessary by the problem of the relation of the Jewish law to Christianity so that faith rather than the works of law might be seen as the actuating principle of Christianity. The letter to the Romans is a systematic exposition and explanation of the gospel. The four epistles written during his imprisonment in Rome were occasioned by the special problems in the churches of Ephesus, Colosse, and Philippi. The personal epistle to Philemon is concerned with the problem of the Christian master and the slave who became a Christian. The three pastoral letters to Timothy and Titus are concerned with the problems facing a young pastor.

It will be noticed that each of these letters grew out of a definite historical crisis in one of Paul's beloved churches. The greatness of these "tracts for the times" is revealed by the fact that the principles that Paul developed to meet emergencies in first-century churches are still relevant to the church in modern times. Human beings face similar problems, and similar principles are useful even if the temporal and spatial environment is different. The Pauline Epistles are of value to any church in the solution of its problems. Paul always balanced theological formulas by practical application.

The Principles of Paul's Thought

No historical discussion of Paul can afford to ignore the basic doctrines that are developed in his letters, particularly in the letter to the Roman church. Christ left no well-defined body of dogma. The formulation of this was to be the work of Paul, guided by the Holy Spirit. This body of theology was not, however, in contrast to the teachings of Christ; rather, it grew out of the teachings and death of Christ; Paul's education at home, in the synagogue, and under Gamaliel; his observation of nature (Rom. 1:19–20); his experience of conversion; his creative mind; and, above all, divine revelation were important in the development of his theology.

Paul's Message

The essence of the Pauline gospel may be simply summarized. Paul realized that happiness and usefulness are basic goals to which all men aspire. Happiness and usefulness in this and the next life are dependent on the achievement of God's favor. God's favor can be granted only to the one who does God's will. Paul and his Jewish compatriots believed that observance of the law of Moses, which was an expression of God's holiness, should guarantee a happy and useful life. However, Paul found to his sorrow that the works of the law only result in the knowledge of sin and leave man helpless to fulfill the will of God as expressed in that law (Rom. 7). The experience on the Damascus road revealed to Paul that not the law but the Cross of Christ is the starting point for spiritual life. Christ, who had kept the Jewish law perfectly, could as perfect man and God offer Himself on the cross on behalf of sinful man and assume the burden of man's sin (Gal. 3:10, 13). People need only accept by faith (Rom. 5:1) the work that Christ has done for them.

Paul's ethical system grew out of this personal union

of the believer with Christ by faith. This vertical relationship is to be balanced by a horizontal relationship in which one is united with fellow believers by Christian love expressed in a moral life (Eph. 1:15; 1 John 3:23). Neither the legalism of Judaism nor the rationalism of Stoicism, but Christian love is to be the spring of Christian conduct. The mystic union of the believer with his Lord is to be the source of love. This life of love involves separation from personal defilement growing out of idol worship, sexual impurity, or drunkenness— the major sins of heathendom. It results, positively, in loving service to others and steadfastness in the matter of personal integrity.

Such a system of ethics did not mean repudiation of the Jewish moral law, but rather it meant its fulfillment on the higher level of love in the family, household, and the state. The high ethical standards of the Christians impressed their pagan neighbors with the greatness of the Christian faith. Paul's own life of selfless service was a revelation to both Jew and Gentile of what God could do in the development of a Christian personality devoted to service for the glory of God and the good of man.

Paul's philosophy of history is closely related to his ethical and theological views. He rejected the cyclic theory of history, which was so characteristic of the ancient world, and the modern theory of indefinite evolutionary progress, in favor of a cataclysmic supernatural view of history that takes into account unregenerate man's failure and God's power to fulfill His divine plan. This view is not limited to nations but encompasses the human race. According to it, progress can come only through spiritual conflict in which man is given strength through the grace of God. Ultimately God will be victor over all the forces of evil that were provisionally defeated on the cross of Calvary by Christ (Rom. 11:36; Eph. 1:10).

Paul as a Polemicist

Paul was never content merely to present Christianity; threats to the purity of Christian doctrine brought him into the fight against the foe. By voice and pen he fought for purity of Christian doctrine in his day. No deficient view of the person or work of Christ escaped his castigation, nor did he fail to try to win the erring one back to the faith.

The problem of the scope and means of salvation was the first difficulty to which Paul addressed himself during the Jerusalem Council at the end of his first missionary journey. The church, born in the bosom of Judaism, had developed into two groups. One group of Jewish Christians with a Pharisaic background believed that Gentiles as well as Jews must keep the law of Moses for salvation. They wanted to make Christianity a particularistic sect of Judaism. The other group realized that salvation came by faith in Christ alone and that the offer of salvation was for all rather than for Jews only, and that by works.

The visit of Judaizers to Antioch, ostensibly with authority from James to preach the former view (Acts 15:24), was the occasion for the meeting at Jerusalem in 49 or 50 to settle this problem. Commissioned by the church at Antioch (Acts 15:2) and assured by revelation (Gal. 2:2), Paul and Barnabas made their way to Jerusalem to the first and, possibly, the most important church council in church history.

They described their activities to a general public meeting of the church (Acts 15:4–5), after which they met with the apostles and elders in a special private meeting to discuss the problem in detail and to try to work out a solution (Acts 15:6; Gal. 2:2–10). This private meeting seems to have been followed by another meeting of the whole church in which a decision was reached that was agreeable to all those present (Acts 15:7–29). The commendation of Paul's work among the Gentiles (Acts 15:25–26; Gal. 2:9) and the freeing of the Gentiles from keeping the Jewish law (Acts 15:19) were the immediate results of the conference. Minor demands to conciliate Jewish believers, such as refraining from eating blood or things strangled, were stated. Gentile converts were also asked to avoid the sins of idolatry and immorality—sins that would be a special temptation to converts from a sinful pagan environment (Acts 15:20–21). It will be clearly seen that these requests had nothing to do with the basic principle of how people are justified. They were designed simply to facilitate good relations between Jewish and Gentile converts to Christianity.

The happenings at the Jerusalem Council revealed Paul's doggedness where a matter of principle was concerned. Not for one moment would he consider the circumcision of Titus at the council (Gal. 2:3), but at the beginning of his second journey, when Timothy became his helper, he had Timothy circumcised (Acts 16:1–3) in order that the lack of this rite might not be a barrier in the presentation of the gospel. Paul was willing to make harmless concessions, such as this one, in order to facilitate his work; but he would not permit Titus to be circumcised at Jerusalem because Gentile freedom from observance of the Jewish ritual law was the principle for which he was fighting.

The liberation of Christianity from observance of the ceremonial Jewish law was the long-range result of the council. Henceforth, faith is the only means by which salvation comes to man. Because this faith is for all peoples, Christianity is freed from the danger of becoming only a sect of Judaism. The new law of love, which leads to the keeping of the Jewish moral law out of love to God rather than out of a sense of duty, becomes the basis for Christian ethics. It is also interesting to note the democratic fashion in which the church met its great problem. The decision was made by the church and its leaders under the guidance of the Holy Spirit. Jewish Christians, who had been saved by faith, were left free to observe the law of Moses as a voluntary task if they so desired.

Christianity must never forget the Jerusalem Council. The same problem was faced by the Reformers, who saw that the Roman church was demanding man-made works in addition to faith as the condition for salvation. Modern liberals with their emphasis on pleasing God by ethical deeds make the same mistake. The problem of the Jerusalem Council is a perennial one, and the principles that were victorious there are principles that have relevance throughout the history of the church.

Paul also faced the challenge of Greek rationalism when he fought an incipient Gnosticism in the church. Some men sought to make the means of salvation *intellectual* as the Jewish Christians had sought to make them *legalistic*. Gnosticism developed with particular danger in the Colossian church.

The Gnostics held to a dualistic philosophy that made a sharp distinction between spirit as good and matter as evil. According to them, the link between pure spirit and evil matter is a hierarchy of celestial beings. Christ is considered one of this hierarchy. Angels are to receive worship because they have a part in this hierarchy (Col. 2:8, 18–19). Salvation is to be achieved mainly by ascetic acts to deny the desires of the material and evil body (Col. 2:14–17, 20–23) and by a special gnosis or knowledge accessible only to the elite among Christians. Faith is relegated to a subordinate position in this system that panders to human pride.

Paul answered this heresy by unqualifiedly asserting the all-sufficiency of Christ as Creator and Redeemer (Col. 1:13–20). Christ is the full manifestation of God and is in no way inferior to God (Col. 1:19; 2:9). Only in this doctrine did Paul feel that man had any assurance of a Savior adequate to meet the problem of sin.

Gnosticism was the first heresy to be met by the church, but it was by no means the last. Error is perennial and usually springs from the same causes in every age. Man's pride in reason and his rationalizing tendency can still lead to heresy as it did in the Colossian church. Retention of the religious heritage of the pre-Christian period in the individual life may lead to a mixture of truth and error with dire consequences for salvation. That was the mistake made by the Judaizers. Misuse or overemphasis of some Scripture may lead to error. Sometimes a leader with mistaken enthusiasm, who seeks to protect the truth, may subvert it. Such was the case of Montanus in the second century.

With such faith and courage, it is little wonder that Paul was able to carry the message of salvation to the Gentile nations of the Roman Empire and to start Christian culture on its triumphant westward march across Europe. He was the unique interpreter of the meaning of Christ's life and death in terms of salvation for sinful man. He kept the faith free from admixture of legalism and rationalism. He worked out the details of organization in the Christian churches and was in constant correspondence with them to help them solve their problems in a Christian manner. As no one else did, Paul realized the cosmic significance of Christ for time and eternity: and, as the "apostle of the nations" (Rom. 11:13; 15:16), he interpreted Christ to the Gentile world.

Christianity Diverges from Judaism

by Mark A. Noll

Mark A. Noll, professor at Wheaton College and author of many books, including *The Scandal of the Evangelical Mind*, discusses events in Judea roughly forty years after the death of Jesus. Noll explains how the Romans' brutal repression of a Jewish rebellion, including the destruction of Jerusalem, pushed the early Christian church to cut its ties to Judaism and expand independently beyond the Mediterranean.

―――――――――――

In A.D. 66, Jewish exasperation with the insensitive rule of Rome at last came to a boil. A long history of strife lay in the background between Jews and the Roman occupiers of Judea. Jewish relations with Greek-speaking settlers, merchants, and imperial officials, who were sheltered by the Roman umbrella, were no better. Rome had frequently raided the temple treasury to make up for what it called unpaid taxes. It had sent Greek-speaking procurators as rulers to Palestine who had neither interest in nor sympathy for Judea or Judaism. It had monopolized positions of wealth and influence. It had pushed the Jewish farmers of the countryside deeper and deeper into debt.

Revolt in Jerusalem

The Jewish revolt began in Caesarea, on the Mediterranean coast about fifty miles northwest of Jerusalem. Greek-speakers celebrated a local legal victory by launching an attack on the Jewish quarters. The Roman army stood by passively as Jews were cut down. When word of these events arrived in Jerusalem, there was an immediate reaction. Although the Jews were divided into many factions, radical voices carried the day. Jews attacked the local garrison, slaughtered its defenders, and appealed for an end of the hated subjugation to Rome. When priests and other more moderate Jewish leaders stopped the mandated ritual sacrifices to the Roman empire, all-out war became inevitable.

Seven years of bloody strife followed. At first the Jewish rebels gained the upper hand. Then, under the tested veteran general Vespasian, Rome sent four legions to discipline its wayward Judean colony. Vespasian advanced cautiously, first securing the Mediterranean ports and then moving slowly against Jerusalem. The noose he was constructing for the Jewish capital relaxed in the summer of 68, when the emperor Nero died, for Vespasian himself was a candidate to succeed him. Events in Rome moved slowly, but eventually Vespasian was handed the palm, and so he left Judea. But this was only a temporary respite. To carry on the job, Vespasian left his son, Titus, who proved just as forceful as his father.

Once again the Roman legions moved toward Jerusalem. Once again the noose tightened. This time there was no relief. In April of the year 70, the siege began. The suffering of those who were trapped in Jerusalem became horrific. In September the most zealous Jewish rebels made their last stand in the temple. Fragmentary sources describing the revolt leave conflicting accounts as to Titus's intentions. Josephus, a former Jewish general who had come over to the Romans in the early days of the revolt, wrote that Titus hoped to save the temple as a gesture of Roman moderation. A later Roman authority, Sulpicius Severus, reported an account from the great Roman historian Tacitus with a different story. This report held that Titus was eager to destroy the temple. Titus's reasoning, as reported by Sulpicius Severus, is particularly noteworthy, for he wanted to eradicate the temple [as quoted by historian and biblical scholar F.F. Bruce] "in order that the Jewish and Christian religions might more completely be abolished; for although these religions were mutually hostile, they had nevertheless sprung from the same founders; the Christians were an offshoot of the Jews, and if the root were taken away the stock would easily perish."

Whether or not Sulpicius Severus got the story right, his comments illuminated a crucial reality about the early history of the Christian church. Titus would go on to wipe out the last remnants of Jewish resistance, including the determined band that held the mountain fortress Masada for nearly three years after the fall of Jerusalem. Later Jewish resistance to Rome would elicit even harsher repression, especially from Emperor Hadrian in response to a revolt in 135. But even before Jerusalem fell and the temple was destroyed in A.D. 70, Titus's observation about the mutual dependence of Christianity and Judaism had become ancient history. While Christianity in its very earliest years may, in fact, have functioned like an appendage of Judaism, by the year 70 it was moving out on its own. That move to independence from Judaism was greatly accelerated by Roman destruction of the Jewish temple and the cessation of the sacrifices that had played such a large role in Jewish worship.

The "Jewishness" of Early Christians

The blows that Vespasian, Titus, Hadrian, and other Roman generals rained upon Jerusalem did not destroy the Christian church. Rather, they liberated the church for its destiny as a universal religion offered to the whole world. Yet from the perspective of the very earliest Christians, Roman decimation of Jerusalem probably seemed like an unspeakable tragedy. Christianity was born in the cradle of Judaism. As indicated by the great meeting reported in Acts 15, the early center of Christianity's communications, organization, and authority was Jerusalem. The first leaders of the church, like James the half-brother of Jesus, who presided over the council in Acts 15, functioned like presidents of a synagogue. The Gospels were written, in large part, as a demonstration of the way that Jesus brought Israel's earlier history to its culmination—Matthew to show that Jesus fulfilled the prophetic promises for the Messiah, Luke to show that Jesus fulfilled the essence of Jewish law, and John to show that the divine revelation to Abraham had culminated in Jesus Christ (John 8:58, "Before Abraham was born, I am"). Several of the early Christian writings were directed to the Jewish diaspora, such as the Epistle of James, which begins, "To the twelve tribes scattered among the nations." Other early Christian writings that would also become part of the New Testament were preoccupied with negotiating the boundaries between Judaism and Christianity. The apostle Paul, especially, argued frequently against those who wanted to maintain the Jewish rite of circumcision as a requirement for salvation. And his interpretations of the Old Testament returned repeatedly to the way in which Jesus' work climaxed God's consistent offer of grace to the Jews. In sum, as historian W.H.C. Frend has written, "All Christianity at this stage [in the apostolic period] was 'Jewish Christianity.' But it was Israel with a difference."

Results of the Rebellion

The great turning point represented by the destruction of Jerusalem was to move Christianity outward, to transform it from a religion shaped in nearly every particular by its early Jewish environment into a religion advancing toward universal significance in the broader reaches of the Mediterranean world, and then beyond. The apostles Peter and Paul were probably martyred in Rome under the emperor Nero about the time that Titus and Vespasian were advancing on Jerusalem. Just a few decades later, Rome would replace Jerusalem as the center of Christian communications and authority. Theological discussion likewise turned rapidly away from problems posed by the system of Jewish morality to issues framed by Hellenistic philosophy or Roman conceptions of order. Already by A.D. 70 Jewish synagogues scattered throughout the Mediterranean, rather than temple worship in Jerusalem, provided the main vehicles for Christian outreach. . . .

The smashing of Jerusalem accelerated a change in perception. To Christians, to Jews, and soon to many others, it was increasingly clear that Rome's disruption of Judaism had pushed the Christian church out on its own. As F.F. Bruce once put it, "In the lands outside Palestine, the decade which ended with the year 70 marked the close of the period when Christianity could be regarded as simply a variety of Judaism. . . . From A.D. 70 onward the divergence of the paths of Jewish Christianity and orthodox Judaism was decisive. . . . Henceforth the main stream of Christianity must make its independent way in the Gentile world."

Now, however, many questions loomed. How would the church define itself? Organize its worship? Find secure authority? Evangelize? Ward off dangerous teaching? In other words, once the "given" framework of Judaism passed away, what would take its place? The three centuries after the fall of Jerusalem provided answers to these questions. We turn now to the means that the church employed to find stability and to sustain its growth in the period after the apostles (that is, the "subapostolic" period). But as we do, it is well to be reminded of how symbolically important was the Roman destruction of Jerusalem. By making it impossible for Judaism to continue in a normal course of development, the Romans also forced great changes upon the Christian church. The turning point of Christian history at Jerusalem in A.D. 70 was the church's emergence on its own. . . .

Problems Faced by the Early Church

Yet in order to expand in this Roman world, the new religion of Christianity needed much more than generally favorable political, social, and religious conditions. The dispersion of Jewish synagogues throughout the Mediterranean might provide a base of operations for Christian missionaries, as the Book of Acts describes for Paul and his colleagues. Yet Christian claims about a "crucified Messiah" or about the existence of non-Jews who became "children of Abraham" by faith (Gal. 3:7) offended Jews deeply and drew determined opposition down upon the church. In a similar fashion, Rome might provide peaceful conditions for travel and the spread of new ideas, but the empire was also jealous and would not stand by patiently when upstarts insisted that, not Caesar, but only Jesus the Christ, should be called Lord. Roman persecution, which flared under the emperors Nero (from A.D. 64), Domitian (from 90), and Marcus Aurelius (in 177) before being exerted systematically by the emperors Decius and Valerian (mid-third century) and Diocletian (start of the fourth century), took deadly aim at the new faith.

Even more serious than religious opposition from Judaism and persecution from Rome, the early church faced a welter of internal uncertainties. Could clear lines be drawn between true worship of Jesus Christ and the era's multitude of Greek, Roman, and Middle Eastern religions that also featured revelations from a high God and appeals for dedicated moral life on earth? Could the intense spiritual life of Christianity be distinguished from the colorful spirituality of groups that modern historians call Gnostic for their reliance on various forms of secret wisdom (gnōiss)? Toward the end of the second century the Christian apologist Irenaeus listed 217 forms of such religions, some of which borrowed liberally from Christian doctrines or practices. Could the church, moreover, succeed in promoting the kind of moral purity that Jesus and the apostles described as appropriate for servants of God? The moral world into which the church was moving was one in which leaders, especially Roman emperors, often indulged in the most degenerate practices, and ordinary people were often more than eager to follow the leader.

Solutions to These Problems

So it was that beset by external foes and menaced by ideas and practices threatening its internal character, the church moved out into the wider world. Once stripped of a Jewish framework by the events involved in the destruction of Jerusalem, how would the church make its way? Answers to these life-threatening challenges could be perceived, at least in outline, within one or two generations after the deaths of the apostles Peter and Paul, which probably occurred under Nero in the years 64–67. By the year 112, Ignatius, leader of the Christian church in Antioch of Syria, could urge fellow believers to "follow the bishop as Jesus Christ followed the father," [as quoted in Henry Bettenson's *Documents of the Christian Church*]. His injunction revealed the emergence of a system of church organization constructed around locally powerful bishops who were assuming the tasks of guiding the faithful in their localities while deliberating with fellow bishops in other places about the general direction of the church.

At least by the time that Ignatius made this reference to bishops, there were also circulating among the expanding Christian congregations two collections of Christian documents—one, the fourfold gospel account of the life of Christ recorded by Matthew, Mark, Luke, and John, the other collection containing copies of ten to thirteen letters from the apostle Paul. It was not long until these two collections would be permanently joined by the Acts of the Apostles to constitute a "new testament" of sacred writings to set alongside the "old testament" of the Hebrew Scriptures and so provide authoritative written guidance for the church.

In roughly the same period that witnessed the evolution of an episcopal system of church organization and a scriptural record of Christ and the meaning of his life, there also began to appear short, concise summaries of what it meant to be a Christian or to join a local congregation. These creeds (from Latin *credo*, "I believe," or *credimus*, "we believe") would prove immensely useful both as a way of marking out the boundaries of Christian faith and as introductions to its character for inquirers or the children of believers.

Along with the episcopate and the canon of Scripture, the early creeds became the anchors that stabilized the church in its earliest subapostolic history. The means by which the church came into its own—after the climactic events in Jerusalem of A.D. 70 and in the face of external and internal pressure—can thus be summarized simply as creed, canon, and episcopacy.

CHAPTER 2

The Rise of the Church (313–1517)

Constantine's Victory Legitimizes Christianity

by David F. Wright

Under the so-called Tetrarchy, or rule of four emperors (285–313), Roman persecution of Christians became severe. The strongest of the emperors, Diocletian, issued a series of harsh decrees beginning in 303 that required Christians to pledge allegiance to the pagan state religion, which gave the emperor the status of a god. The Christian clergy was discredited, and Christians were variously expelled, imprisoned, or executed. Then in 312, Constantine, son of the tetrarch Constantius, won a battle for control of the empire after having a vision of a cross, intertwined with Greek letters representing the name of Christ, and the phrase "Under this sign, you will conquer." Constantine is said to have put this symbol on his armies' shields, and credited his victory to the Christian God. In the following selection, David F. Wright, dean of the Faculty of Divinity at the University of Edinburgh, explains Constantine's conversion, his subsequent decisions reversing the persecution, and the impact of his decisions on the Christian church.

Constantine has earned a place in history for many reasons—not least because he brought to an end the persecutions of Christians by the pagan Roman Empire. A concordat agreed to with his fellow emperor, Licinius, at Milan in 313 granted "both to Christians and to all others full authority to follow whatever worship each person has desired. . . . Every one of those who have a common wish to follow the religion of the Christians may from this moment freely and unconditionally proceed to observe the same without any annoyance or disquiet." In retrospect, the agreement forms one of the major watersheds in the history of Christianity, bidding farewell to the age of the martyrs and presaging the era of the Christian Empire.

What sort of man was he, this Constantine "the Great," the first emperor of Rome to come out unambiguously on the side of the Christian church? How significant were the so-called Edict of Milan and the other actions he took as patron of the church? How truly Christian was he himself?

Early Days

Constantine was born on February 27, probably in 272, in the military town of Naissus—modern Nis in eastern Yugoslavia. His father, Constantius, was an army officer; his mother, Helena, was a woman of lowly origins whom Constantius later (probably by 290) found it prudent to divorce as his political aspirations took shape. Not much is known for certain about their religious attitudes. Helena became a Christian—and one of outstanding piety—only after her famous son's conversion. Constantius enforced without enthusiasm only the first of the anti-Christian measures of the Great Persecution in Britain and Gaul (France)—the sector of the Empire he took charge of in 293 as a junior emperor (Caesar).

One of his children by his second wife was named Anastasia, from the Greek word for "resurrection," which implies pro-Christian sympathies going beyond mere tolerance. Eusebius later portrayed him as a worshiper of the one true God, but not in unmistakably Christian terms. The evidence suggests that Constantine could have acquired from his father a predisposition to take a serious look at Christianity when the opportunity offered.

As the son of a Caesar and hence potentially an emperor himself, Constantine spent a dozen years (from about 293 to 305) in the East in the court of Diocletian, the senior emperor (Augustus), and Galerius, his deputy (Caesar). Constantine could be regarded both as an imperial apprentice and as a hostage (ensuring the good conduct of his father). He passed the time partly in Diocletian's palace at Nicomedia (modern Izmit, Turkey, not far from the eastern shore of the Bosporus) and partly in the field on military campaigns. Constantine's religious development in these formative years is largely hidden from us, but he could hardly have been unaware of the Christians in an area of the Empire where they were thickest. The ranks of Diocletian's officials and perhaps even his close family included some Christians, and the church building in Nicomedia was easily visible from the palace windows.

Taking Over

The Great Persecution initiated from Nicomedia in 303–304 must have been highly distasteful to Constantine. In circumstances that scholars debate (did he flee at the first opportunity and take steps to prevent pursuit?), Constantine left Nicomedia soon after Galerius succeeded Diocletian (as Augustus) on May 1, 305, and made his way to Britain to his father—now also a senior emperor (Augustus). On Constantine's father's death at York on July 25, 306, his troops saluted Constantine as Augustus in his place. This was scarcely a regular (though not uncommon) route to the imperial throne, and Constantine would have to vindicate his right to rule on the battlefield.

To cut a tangled story short, on October 28, 312, he defeated Maxentius at the Milvian Bridge, a dozen miles up the Tiber from Rome, and thereby became sole master of the Western Empire. Twelve years later, he finally routed the forces of Licinius and became "Ruler of the Entire Globe"—or at least of the whole Empire.

Favoring the Christians

From the winter of 312–313 onward—that is, from soon after his triumphant entry into Rome as controller of the West—Constantine's actions reveal increasing favor toward the Christian church. During those months he sent three letters to Carthage (near modern Tunis), the capital of Roman North Africa. The first ordered the Roman governor to restore to "the catholic church of the Christians in any city" all the property it had formerly owned, irrespective of its present owner. The second letter informed the bishop of Carthage that funds would soon reach him for distribution to "certain specific ministers of the lawful and most holy catholic religion," and also assured him of protection against elements disruptive to the catholic church. The third letter, again to the governor, exempted clergy from the burdens of inherited responsibilities as local councillors. The reason given is highly significant: "The setting at nought of divine worship . . . has brought great dangers upon public affairs, and its lawful restoration and preservation have bestowed the greatest good fortune on the Roman name and singular prosperity on all the affairs of mankind (for it is the divine providence which bestows these blessings)." The clergy, "when they render supreme service to the Deity, . . . confer incalculable benefit on the affairs of the state."

Religious Convictions

Sentiments like these resonate throughout Constantine's letters and edicts. They reveal a deeply religious man who believed that the well-being of the Empire was dependent on God, and that God would prosper the fortunes of the Empire so long as he was truly worshiped by its inhabitants. This true worship (so Constantine held, with ever-sharpening clarity) was the worship offered by the Christian church, and the true God was the God of the Christians.

How Constantine came by these controlling religious convictions has long been disputed. Two Christian writers, Lactantius and Eusebius, had direct contact with Constantine in later years. They write that on the eve of the Battle of the Milvian Bridge, Constantine had a dream (Lactantius) or a vision (Eusebius) that convinced him to enter the fray, trusting in the Christians' God, and to display a distinctively Christian emblem. The veracity of these accounts is, in the last resort, beyond corroboration. Nevertheless, they speak, in however embellished a form, of a decisive shift in religious allegiance—a conversion—and this is acknowledged today by eminent Roman historians, like Ramsay MacMullen and Timothy Barnes, who have no ecclesiastical axe to grind. As Norman H. Bayne wrote, Constantine's action in confronting Maxentius "is more explicable if

Constantine was convinced that the Christian God had assured him victory."

It must be stressed, though, that the genuineness of Constantine's pro-Christian stance does not depend on the historicity of the dream and the vision. It is writ unmistakably large in his words and deeds from shortly after the decisive victory. This consideration, for those who carry no prejudice against divine communications through dreams and visions, may properly count in favor of their authenticity in Constantine's case.

Superficial Faith?

Constantine probably never gained a good grounding in Christian doctrine, however. As late as 324 he could regard the momentous divide opening up between the heretic Arius and his opponents as "a small and very insignificant question." Only gradually and never frequently does he speak of "Christ" and "our Savior" rather than simply of "God" or, in more impersonal terms, "the divine power," "providence," "the supreme Deity," etc.

Constantine was baptized only after the onset of his final illness, not many days before his death on Pentecost, May 22, 337. But if only then do we see him as a penitent (and delayed baptism was the norm at the time), the explanation lies largely in a circumstance too often forgotten or minimized by critics who depict him as a hypocrite, an impostor, or even a monster. It is simply this: Constantine was the emperor of Rome, the civil and military (and religious) head of the Empire. Our sources give us little access to the private Constantine. His letters and edicts are all official utterances. It is perhaps more remarkable that they make his religious convictions so clear than that they speak so little of Jesus Christ in terms of personal devotion.

Intermingled Paganism

Constantine's religion is from first to last that of an autocratic ruler of an empire secured by military might—and still overwhelmingly pagan. If pagan elements did not disappear from his coinage immediately after his conversion, that should scarcely surprise us. Constantine's legislative and executive actions can be fairly understood only when judged not anachronistically, against some ideal portrait of the Christian monarch (there were, after all, no precedents, no available role models, to guide a Roman emperor who was also a Christian), but historically, in a brutal age that took harsh retributive punishments for granted. And so his wife and eldest son had to die for offenses of treason. Not in vain did this Constantine bear the sword.

Yet in many details a Christian inspiration can be glimpsed in his legal enactments—for example, on the treatment of prisoners and slaves, on the status-less underclass of Roman society, on the exposure of surplus children, on celibacy and marriage and extra-marital infidelity.

But it is important not to make Constantine out to be more consistently Christian than he was. His conversion was not accompanied by a sharp break with his former paganism. Rather, a transition is discernible from the worship of the divine Sun to the service of the one true Christian God. When, in 321, he made the first day of the week a holiday, he described it as the day of the sun (but so do Christians today!). Christian regard for the Lord's Day, however, alone motivated this ruling.

Consequences

Few individuals have set as many precedents as Constantine. He launched the church on its way to becoming the official, established religion of the Roman Empire—a journey it completed half a century later under Theodosius the Great. And by founding Constantinople as a "New Rome," a Christian Rome, he laid the foundations for the noble Christian civilization of the Byzantine or East Roman Empire that would survive for a millennium after the Empire in the West had disintegrated. By his patronage Constantine aligned the former church of the martyrs—persecuted, powerless, and pacifist—with the military might and earthly glory of the state. Christianity would never be the same again.

Soon the wars of the Empire became holy wars; church leaders looked for civil sanctions to back up their ecclesiastical judgments (the Council of Nicaea deposed Arius; Constantine exiled him); rulers began to convene synods of church leaders and to influence or intimidate their proceedings; the church hierarchies learned how to invoke state coercion against heretics and schismatics, and they came to control increasing property and wealth. Persecution soon resumed of Christians by Christians, of pagans by Christians, of Jews and Moslems by Christians.

Yet if blame must be apportioned, much belongs not to Constantine but to those church leaders who not only, it seems, failed to teach him any better, but even, like Eusebius above all, constructed an extravagant theology of the Christian emperor that made him almost the earthly embodiment of divine power.

Augustine's Conversion Leads to the Development of Key Christian Principles

by C.W. McPherson

C.W. McPherson, rector of Trinity–St. Paul Episcopal Church in New Rochelle, New York, explores the vital importance of Augustine to Christianity as theologian, philosopher, and author.

Augustine . . . seems to shed light in any direction: ethical, theological, devotional and spiritual, philosophical, practical. He appears throughout the Roman Breviary and the Anglican Prayer Book. Protestants claim him as the key to theological liberation, while Roman Catholics claim him as the source and substance for everything Thomas Aquinas reasoned through seven centuries later. I could not avoid him when pursuing doctoral studies in Old English literature, so enormously had he influenced early Medieval Western thought and art (and as I was writing my dissertation, the novelist Anthony Burgess published a novel based on Augustine's adventures against the Pelagians). I have done two close studies of Augustine—one, of his conferences written shortly after his baptism; the other, of

C.W. McPherson, "Augustine Our Contemporary," *Cross Currents*, Spring/ Summer 2000, pp. 170–74. Copyright © 2000 by the Association for Religion and Intellectual Life. Reproduced by permission.

his late and extraordinary theological study, *On the Trinity.* I cannot avoid him now, as a parish priest, since his simple injunction to "become what you are" so powerfully and paradoxically expresses our relationship to our baptismal vows. . . .

What is it, then, about Augustine that makes him so useful, so relevant? What gives this orthodox, catholic theologian, so firmly embraced by Christian tradition, relevance in an era which seems to be witnessing the dissolution of that tradition? How does a fourth-century bishop, in a relatively obscure cure (. . . he was merely one among many North African bishops at the time, and his see [area of bishop's authority], Hippo, was by no means especially eminent), speak to the twenty-first century? What makes Augustine our contemporary?

Augustine Advanced Key Principles

My first suggestion is simple but not obvious: Augustine's era mirrors our own—more than any subsequent era—and that alone gives his thought a particular usefulness for us. I realize this claim has been made for various historic periods, but I am convinced that the age of anxiety which the fourth and fifth centuries of the common era witnessed offers our most complete, valid, and instructive historical precedent. The world of the late Roman Empire knew the tremendous advantages of a colossal network of transportation and communication, of advanced technological achievement, of internationalism, and of cultural, intellectual, and theological pluralism. It also experienced the concomitant disadvantages of a dislocation of values, internecine warfare and random violence, political corruption and revolution, ethnic and racial tensions, new disease, and existential despair. This is Augustine's context, and it is also ours; we understand that world in a way our more immediate forbears could not possibly.

Thus we find Augustine speaking to us with a relevance that can seem almost startling. *The City of God*, his most famous and influential work, is replete with this quality. Augustine does not write theoretically and hypothetically here; he responds to the moral and theological concerns of a world racked by pillage and destruction, random and chaotic violence, mutilation and murder. His parenthetical advice to victims of rape, indeed, runs like a leitmotiv throughout the initial chapters. Its basic theme is theodicy: justification of the ways of God to humankind, attempts to answer the question of innocent suffering. Augustine knew that serious inquirers in the early fifth century would demand this of a philosophical theologian, and we who have closed the twentieth century make the same demand. He writes, Augustine says, "first, because many are disturbed in mind when they observe how, in the daily round of life, God's gifts and man's brutalities oftentimes fall indifferently and indiscriminately to the lot of both the good and the bad," and the entire work, with its very careful and detailed vision of history theologically interpreted, is his response to that disturbance. We may not accept every argument he marshals—"by the same fire gold gleams and straw smokes"—but the overarching thesis, that happiness is the product of meaningful existence, not of pleasant happenstance, and its corollary, that suffering can be accepted with dignity when necessary rather than resented and feared, must remain compelling.

Compelling for all serious thinkers, not just for fellow theists. Augustine wrote for agnostics and nihilists, for thoughtful classical conservatives demanding a return to pagan values and pagan gods, for disciples of any of the bewildering variety of philosophical schools and sects that flourished in the late empire, for rival religionists, as well as for practicing Christians. This gives his work a philosophical integrity lacking in many subsequent theologians, who wrote within a strictly Christian context for a specifically Christian readership. Consider for example his reflections on time and creation. In contrast to many Christian thinkers, who sought to establish a history of creation and offer a time scale, Augustine offers a relativistic argument:

> What is made in time is made after one period of time and before another, namely, after a past and before a future time. But, there could have been no past time, since there was nothing created by whose movements and change time could be measured. The fact is that the world was made simultaneously with time, if, with creation, motion and change began. (XI.6, 202)

We, who have been taught to understand time in quite similar philosophical language, read this not only with understanding but with sympathy—it resonates with us. We respond similarly to his almost offhand treatment of the biblical "days" of creation: "it is difficult, perhaps impossible, to think—let alone explain in words—what they mean."

Augustine's Role in Exploring the Inner Life

Second, Augustine exhibits an interiority, an emphasis on the reality of the inner life, the adventures of the mind, which is on the one hand the culmination of both his platonic heritage and his biblical tradition, yet on the other hand very familiar for us, heirs of modern psychology and modern literature. The most obvious example of course is the *Confessions*, an unprecedented account of the inner life, which traces the subtlest motions of thought, will, and feeling. Consider the famous episode of the theft of the pears:

"If the crime of theft which I committed that night as a boy of sixteen were a living thing, I could speak to it and ask what it was that I loved in it. It had no beauty because it was a robbery. It is true that the pears we stole had beauty, but it was not the pears that my unhappy soul desired. I had plenty of my own, better than those, and I only picked them so that I might steal. For no sooner had I picked them than I threw them away, and tasted nothing but my own sin, which I relished and enjoyed. If any part of one of those pears passed my lips, it was the sin that gave it flavour."

This sort of introspection is unprecedented. Augustine subjects not only his reasoning, his processes of thought, but, as we see in even this short passage, his feelings and the movements of his will to a microscopic recollection and analysis (the work is also rich with many classic passages of simple tenderness and authenticity of feeling). It was to prove enormously helpful for countless Christians making an examination of conscience over the centuries, but we are especially familiar with this sort of thing. In this, Augustine's modern intellectual descendants were Freud on the one hand and Joyce and Proust on the other.

The *Confessions* is, moreover, merely the best-known example of Augustine's work in this mode. Many of his hundreds of surviving works exhibit the same reflexive interiority. Most striking perhaps is the *De Trinitate*, which he began at the turn of the fifth century. This fifteen-volume work is his most theologically innovative, for in it he uses the same sort of introspection he had used in the *Confessions* to prove, not the existence of God, but the existence of the trinitarian, Christian God. Augustine leads the reader through a slow, inward spiraling tour of his own consciousness, or of the human mind, and claims that, along the way, we find a triune dynamic of mind which suggests the imprint of the trinity as surely as the design of the heavens suggests a divine designer. Here Augustine certainly stands out from the tradition, which almost always regards the trinitarian aspect of God as the exclusive province of revealed theology. Historically, moreover, I sense that there has always been a certain uneasiness associated with this particular work. Yet its very theological inwardness makes it particularly attractive in our theologically ecumenical age.

Augustine's Ability to Combine Interests

The third aspect of Augustine's work which commends him to us is actually one he shared with many Christian writers who preceded him—but few who followed. It can be approached through this question: what was Augustine? Was he a philosopher or theologian or teacher within the spiritual tradition? Are his books intellectual exercises, or doctrinal, or devotional? Is his primary concern the existence or nature of God, or ethics, or ontology, or epistemology, or morals, or history? The answer, of course, is all of these. Augustine is the only figure who appears substantially in Louis Bouyer's comprehensive history of Christian spirituality, in Frederick Copleston's comprehensive history of philosophy, in Jaroslav Pelikan's history of theology, and even in Eric

Auerbach's classic literary essay, *Mimesis.*

This is not merely a matter of a single person's interest in a number of areas. Augustine combines these disciplines in each of his books. In his *On Free Choice of the Will,* for example, Augustine presents a closely reasoned, dialectical argument on the subjects of volition and predestination, derived ultimately from Plato's *Euthyphro;* at the same time, he appeals consistently to scriptures, offers ascetical advice, and concludes with a beatific vision:

"So great is the beauty of justice, so great the joy of eternal light, of the unchangeable Truth and Wisdom, that even though a man were not allowed to remain in its light for longer than a day, yet in comparison with this he would rightly and properly despise a life of innumerable years spent in the delight of temporal goods. Indeed, the following is neither false nor trivial: 'Far better is one day in thy courts than thousands.' Yet it is also possible to understand this in another sense, namely that the 'thousands of days' may be interpreted to represent the transience of time, while the term 'one day' represents the immutability of eternity."

This sort of thing is in itself no ordinary achievement: very few Christian writers, making reference to the Bible on every page, are at the same time quite intelligible to anyone outside the tradition through their sheer logical power (Aquinas, for example, is not). The vast apologetic of the *City of God* similarly makes constant reference to scriptures without once losing the thread of the logic; it simultaneously offers observations on philosophy, history, ethics, even mathematics, all of which contribute to the argument. Many of Augustine's works are, like the *Confessions* (and like the later works of the next great philosopher-theologian, Anselm), cast in the form of a vast prayer, addressed to God.

Augustine makes genuine contributions to several fields not because he is multifaceted so much as because his thought is seamless. That, too, appeals to us; that attracts us. From the impulse in physics to find a general field theory to the popular use of the word *holistic*, we have evidence of a yearning for the comprehensive, catholic vision, a frustration with the compartmentalization and departmentalization which have so characterized modern thought. Not only mathematics and the natural sciences, but philosophy, literature, and theology have become intelligible to specialists only, closed disciplines; by contrast, for all his erudition and comprehensiveness, Augustine represents a fundamental openness and simplicity we find immensely attractive. Whether postmodern philosophy or theology will achieve a comprehensive vision remains to be seen; Augustine certainly did.

Jerome Translates the Bible: The Authoritative Scriptures of the Western World

by Bruce M. Metzger

The stories and poems in the Old Testament were originally passed down orally. Later, they were written in
Hebrew. Around 250 B.C., Jewish scholars translated the
Hebrew writings into Greek. This translation, known as
the Septuagint, was the Bible that the early Christian
church used. The New Testament was likewise written
in Greek.

Jerome, probably the greatest Christian scholar in
the world, was asked by Pope Damasus to prepare a
new translation of the Bible, partly because many subject peoples in the Roman Empire knew no Greek. Earlier scholars had tried translating the Bible into Latin,
which was becoming the standard language of the
Western Empire, but these early translators' linguistic
expertise was limited. Damasus asked Jerome to apply
his superior knowledge of Greek to a new translation.

In the following excerpt, Bruce M. Metzger, professor
of New Testament language and literature at Princeton
Theological Seminary and an expert in ancient biblical
manuscripts, discusses these early translations and the

need to create a clear revision in Latin. He explains how Jerome's translation, using Latin, Greek, and Hebrew sources, became the recognized scripture of the Western world for a thousand years.

————————————

It would be difficult to overestimate the importance of the influence exerted by the Latin versions of the Bible and particularly by Jerome's Latin Vulgate [literally, common or general]. Whether one considers the Vulgate from a purely secular point of view, with its pervasive influence on the development of Latin into Romance languages, or whether one has in view only the specifically religious influence, the extent of its penetration into all areas of Western culture is almost beyond calculation. The theology and the devotional language typical of the Roman Catholic Church were either created or transmitted by the Vulgate. Both Protestants and Roman Catholics are heirs of terminology that Jerome either coined or baptized with fresh significance—words such as salvation, regeneration, justification, sanctification, propitiation, reconciliation, inspiration, Scripture, sacrament, and many others.

History of Previous Latin Translations

The historian of the Latin versions of the Bible is confronted with difficult and disputed problems, not least of which are the questions when, where, and by whom the earliest Latin rendering was made. Because the language used by the church at Rome was Greek until the mid-third century, the Old Latin versions would not have originated there, but within those early Christian communities that used Latin. Probably by the end of the second century A.D., Old Latin versions of the Scriptures were in circulation in North Africa. In Carthage, Tertullian (ca. 150–ca. 220) and Cyprian (ca. 200–258) quoted long sections of both Testaments in Latin. Since one finds numerous and far-reaching differences between quotations of the same passages, it is obvious that there was no one uniform rendering; some books were apparently translated a number of times, and no single translator worked on all of the books. The Old Testament was not translated from the Hebrew but was based, it appears, on [Greek translations from 275–100 B.C.]. In this way, Western churches became familiar with the [non-Hebrew, or added] books of the Old Testament.

Noteworthy Old Latin readings frequently agree with the Greek [and Syriac versions of the Gospels]. On the whole, the African form of the Old Latin presents the larger divergences from the generally received text, and the European the smaller. The diversity among the Old Latin witnesses is probably to be accounted for by the assumption that scribes, instead of copying the manuscripts mechanically, allowed themselves considerable freedom in incorporating their own and others' traditions. In other words, the Old Latin was a living creation, constantly growing.

The roots of the Old Latin versions are doubtless to be found in the practice of the double reading of Holy Scripture during divine services, first in the Greek text and then in the vernacular tongue. In the written form, the translation would at times have been interlinear; later on, manuscripts were prepared with two columns of text, sometimes arranged in shorter or longer lines (called *cola* and *commata*) for ease of phrasing during the public reading of the lessons.

The pre-Jerome translations in general lack polish and are often painfully literal. The Gospels stand in the sequence of Matthew, John, Luke, and Mark in the Old Latin manuscripts *a, b, d, e, ff, q, r*. Here and there one finds noteworthy additions to the text. For example, in Matthew 3:16 the Old Latin manuscript *a* states that when Jesus was baptized, "a tremendous light flashed forth from the water, so that all who were present feared." Old Latin manuscripts give various names to the two robbers who were crucified with Jesus, and Mark's account of Jesus' resurrection is expanded in Old Latin manuscript *k* at 16:4 with the following: "But suddenly at the third hour of the day there was darkness over the whole circle of the earth, and angels descended from the heavens, and as he [the Lord] was rising in the glory of the living God, at the same time they ascended with him; and immediately it was light."

By the close of the fourth century, there was such a confusing diversity among Latin manuscripts of the New Testament that Augustine lamented, "Those who translated the Scriptures from Hebrew into Greek can be counted, but the Latin translators are out of all number. For in the early days of the faith, everyone who happened to gain possession of a Greek manuscript [of the New Testament] and thought he had any facility in both languages, however slight that might have been, attempted to make a translation."

As a consequence, there grew up a welter of diverse Latin translations. Among them three types or families of texts gradually developed; Cyprian (d. 258) represents the African text, Irenaeus (ca. 130–ca. 200) of southern Gaul represents the European, and Augustine (d. 430) the Italian. Characteristic of each family are certain renderings; for example, as a translation of the

Greek word *phōs* ("light"), the African family prefers *lumen*, the European *lux;* for the Greek *dokimazō*, the African prefers *clarificare*, the European *glorificare.*

Jerome and the Pope

In these circumstances, the stage was set for the most decisive series of events in the whole history of the Latin Bible. In the year 383, Pope Damasus urged Jerome (ca. 342–420), the most learned Christian scholar of his day, to produce a uniform and dependable text of the Latin Scriptures; he was not to make a totally new translation but to revise a text of the Bible in use at Rome. Jerome's first inclination was to say "No, thank you" to the pope's invitation. He wrote:

> You urge me to revise the Old Latin version, and, as it were, to sit in judgment on the copies of the Scriptures that are now scattered throughout the world; and, inasmuch as they differ from one another, you would have me decide which of them agree with the original. The labor is one of love, but at the same time it is both perilous and presumptuous—for in judging others I must be content to be judged by all. . . . Is there anyone learned or unlearned, who, when he takes the volume in his hands and perceives that what he reads does not suit his settled tastes, will not break out immediately into violent language and call me a forger and profane person for having the audacity to add anything to the ancient books, or to make any changes or corrections in them?

Two factors, however, prompted Jerome to risk incurring such opprobrium. The first factor, as he related in a dedicatory epistle to Damasus setting forth the occasion and scope of the undertaking, was the command laid upon him by the supreme pontiff. The second was

the shocking diversity among the Old Latin manuscripts, there being, as he wrote, "almost as many forms
of text as there are manuscripts."

Jerome was born at Strido, a town in Dalmatia near
the Adriatic coast, the son of moderately well-to-do
Christian parents. His early training was such as to fit
him admirably for work as translator, for he received a
first-class education in grammar and rhetoric at Rome
under the illustrious teacher Aelius Donatus, of whom
he always spoke with great respect. Jerome applied
himself with diligence to the study of rhetoric and attended the law courts to hear the best pleaders of the
day. He became familiar with the Latin classics and
studied Plautus and Terence, Sallust, Lucretius, Horace,
Virgil, Persius, and Lucan, with commentaries on them
by Donatus and others. These developed his feeling for
literary style, and he became a follower of Ciceronian
traditions.

In the Greek classics, Jerome was less thoroughly at
home. Indeed, it appears that he did not learn Greek at
all until he went to Antioch in 373–74, when he was in
his late twenties. He shows some acquaintance with
Hesiod, Sophocles, Herodotus, Demosthenes, Aristotle,
Theophrastus, and Gregory of Nazianzus.

His scholarly tools also came to include the Hebrew
language. This he learned with great labor in his ma-
ture years, first from a converted but anonymous Jew
during Jerome's five years of ascetic seclusion in the
Syrian desert of Chalcis (374–79) and afterwards in
Bethlehem (about 385) from the Palestinian Rabbi bar-
Anina, who, through fear of the Jews, visited him by
night. Although Jerome's knowledge of Hebrew was de-
fective, it was much greater than that of Origen,
Ephraem Syrus, and Epiphanius, the only other church

fathers who knew Hebrew at all. Such was the philolog-
ical training of the man who was destined to fix the literary form of the Bible of the entire Western Church.

His Translations

Jerome was a rapid worker. Within a year, he finished
his version of the Gospels. There is still some doubt as
to whether he worked alone or with helpers. In a letter
to the pope, he explained his procedure. He altered the
Old Latin text, he said, only when it seemed absolutely
necessary, retaining in other cases what had become familiar phraseology. This principle, though by no means
rigorously observed throughout, explains inconsistencies in practice (e.g., "high priest" is usually translated
in Matthew and Luke by *princeps sacerdotum*, in Mark
by *summus sacerdos*, and in John by *pontifex*). Jerome's
work on the rest of the New Testament was not quite so
thorough; several scholars, in fact, have supposed that
it was done by someone else, perhaps by Jerome's follower Rufinus the Syrian.

Among the Old Testament books, Jerome turned his
attention first to the Psalter. He made two versions of
the Old Latin version of the Psalms by comparing it
with the Greek Septuagint. These are known as the Roman (384) and Gallican (387–90) Psalters, because they
were introduced into Rome and Gaul respectively.
Jerome's final revision of the Psalter was made from the
Hebrew, but it never attained general use or popularity.

About the time Jerome produced his Gallican Psalter,
he also revised the Latin text of some of the other
books of the Old Testament with reference to [an important Greek translation]. This work, however, did not
satisfy Jerome's scholarly standards, and he resolved to

undertake a more thorough revision on the basis of the Hebrew original. This great work occupied him from about the year 390 to 404, and separate books or groups of books were published as they were completed. Whether he managed to complete the entire Old Testament is not clear; at any rate, what is known as the Vulgate translation is far from being a uniform piece of work throughout.

Of course the Old Latin rendering, made from the Septuagint, contained the additional books that over the years had been incorporated into manuscripts of the Greek version of the Old Testament. Jerome's high regard, however, for the [Hebrew text] led him to set the books that found a place in the Hebrew canon on a higher level than those that did not. In this way, he anticipated the Reformers' distinction between "canonical" and "apocryphal." Jerome's work on the latter books was by no means as thorough as on the others. Tobit he translated in one day, Judith in one night, both of which he dictated to a scribe in Latin. Other deuterocanonical [apocryphal] books remain "untranslated," that is, without revision of the Old Latin text.

The apprehension Jerome expressed to Pope Damasus that he would be castigated for tampering with Holy Writ was not unfounded. His revision of the Latin Bible provoked both criticism and anger, sometimes extraordinarily vehement. Augustine, who was himself not too happy with Jerome's preference for the Hebrew original of the Old Testament over the Greek Septuagint (which Augustine regarded as an inspired version), reports an account of tumult that erupted in a North African church at Oea (modern Tripoli) during the reading of a Scripture lesson from the Book of Jonah in Jerome's unfamiliar rendering. When the congregation heard that Jonah took shelter from the sun under some ivy (*hedera*), with one accord they shouted, "Gourd, gourd" (*cucurbita*), until the reader reinstated the old word lest there be a general exodus of the congregation!

For his part, Jerome defended his work with forthright vigor, referring on occasion to his detractors as "two-legged asses" or "yelping dogs"—persons who "think that ignorance is identical with holiness." In the course of time, however, opposition to the revision subsided, and the superior accuracy and scholarship of Jerome's version gave it the victory. It was a clear case of the survival of the fittest.

For nearly a thousand years, the Vulgate was used as the recognized text of Scripture throughout western Europe. It also became the basis of pre-Reformation vernacular Scriptures, such as Wycliffe's English translation in the fourteenth century, as well as the first printed Bibles in German (1466), Italian (1471), Cataláin (1478), Czech (1488), and French (1530).

Benedict's Monastic Rule Brings Continuity of Purpose to Monasteries

by Lewis Browne

In the following selection, Lewis Browne, author of several books on Christianity, Judaism, and other religions, explains the origins of Christian monasticism and the work of Benedict of Nursia (480–547), the Christian saint whose exemplary life as a solitary monk led followers to establish religious communities organized according to his Rule, a written guide for monks' conduct and domestic duties. Bound by common routines and dedication to work, simplicity, obedience, and prayer, Benedictine communities thrived throughout Europe. The stability and continuity provided by the Rule made monasteries vital conservatories of instruction, writing, and scholarship, as well as centers of Christian worship, during the Middle Ages.

In the third century an intense disquiet began to make itself felt in certain Christian circles. It was no organized revolt like that which Montanus had led a century earlier, but rather a sporadic revulsion, leaderless, and for the most part negative in spirit. Isolated individuals be-

Lewis Browne, *Since Calvary*. New York: Macmillan, 1931.

gan to grow restive in the congregations and murmur against the trend the Church was taking. They recalled the tradition that Jesus had praised those who made themselves "eunuchs for the Kingdom of Heaven's sake," and that he had told the rich young man, "If you would be perfect, go, sell your property and give the money to the poor." And they began to complain because these teachings were no longer being followed in the congregations. At first they complained with hesitancy, for the persecutions were still harrying their brethren. But with the coming of Constantine and the establishment of Christianity as a state institution, these protestants began to grow more clamorous. They could see that the ethical teachings were being forgotten, and only the sacerdotal elements were surviving. And this seemed to them a betrayal of the very essence of Christianity. The Church, they cried, had not been founded as a mere agency for cheap salvation; Christ had intended it to be a communion of saints.

Nor were they content simply to proclaim this doctrine; they sought to carry it out in their own lives. Increasing numbers of Christians began to dedicate themselves to celibacy and willful poverty, striving by their example to lead the entire Church back to its pristine austerity. . . .

The Hermits

The first historic character to resort to this measure was an earnest young Christian named Anthony, who took up his abode in the wilderness of southern Egypt toward the end of the third century. . . .

By the fourth century there were hermits to be found in the deserts and forests and mountain fastnesses throughout the empire. Some of them must have been stark lunatics, and others were probably neurotic individuals craving a chance for self-expression. They vied with each other in endurance much as poor boys and girls in our day will vie with each other in "marathon dances" and other such absurd contests calculated to attract attention. St. Jerome assures us that he once saw a monk who for thirty years had lived exclusively on crumbs of barley bread and muddy water, and another who stayed continually in a hole, never washing, never changing his tunic till it fell away in pieces, and who starved himself till his skin was "like pumice stone" and his eyes were almost blind. . . .

The favorite lairs of these sorry masochists were the deserted dens of wild animals, or dry wells, or ruined cemeteries. In Mesopotamia a whole sect of them came to be known as the "Grazers" because they never dwelt under a roof but roamed about half-naked over the mountain sides and lived off the herbage like cattle. . . .

Flight from the World

Such creatures were, of course, exceptional—but only in degree, not in kind. Save for a rare soul like old St. Poemen, who tried to teach his followers that their aim should be to destroy their passions, not their bodies, the ascetics regarded the maddest of their kind as the noblest. If they themselves did not all become St. Simeons and St. Marys, it was solely because they lacked the fortitude. They contented themselves with the less vicious mortifications, dwelling not by themselves in caves or on pillars, but in groups in monasteries. Of such monastics there were many thousands by the end of the fourth century. St. Jerome informs us that in his day—he died in the year 420—some fifty thousand monks used to assemble for the Easter festivals; and his contemporary, Rufinus, declares in his *Historia Eremitica* that the monastic population in Egypt was nearly equal to that of the cities. No doubt the evil conditions of the time had much to do with the popularity of asceticism, for, since hunger was already a necessity, it was comforting to make it a virtue. Whatever the reason, however, the flight from the world began to take on the aspect of an epidemic during these sorry centuries. From Egypt the movement spread southward into Ethiopia, eastward to Persia, northward to the Black Sea, and westward to Italy, Gaul, and Britain, and especially Ireland.

Monasteries

The cloister was in the Middle Ages what the laboratory is in our day—the institutional expression of the spirit of its age. The one may seem grotesque to us, and the other palpably natural; but that is only because the intellectual climate has changed in the intervening centuries. In medieval times the monastery was not a mere convenience but a necessity. It was in fact as well as name a "retreat" from a world grown hateful to mankind. A vast empire had collapsed, dragging with it an order of existence; and the race was left in terror. Gone were the old amenities and securities; now there was naught save hate and dread. And the finest of the race, the most sensitive souls, could not endure it. To dream of redeeming the world was no longer possible; things had gone too far for that. Dreaming of any sort was well-nigh impossible; it was a time only for nightmares. For this life was not the only affliction; even worse was the dread of the life to come. Heaven, which had seemed very close to the Christians in the excitement of the missionizing days, had since receded into the distance. Now Hell was the nearer prospect. The world had grown gray with the breath of the theologians, and the dearest wish of men was not so much to reach God as to escape the Devil.

That was why men flocked to the cloisters. They were panic-stricken lest death overtake them while still in sin and plunge them into the eternal fires of Hell. They sought to isolate themselves from this guilt-infested world and live a life of otherworldly virtue. They searched the Scriptures and read of the Way urged by Jesus; and in that Way they tried with all their desperate might to go. The sacraments in which the commonalty of Christians put their trust seemed not enough for the extremists. Indeed, monasticism was at first very largely an unsacerdotal movement. The anchorites who fled into the wilderness cut themselves off from all chance of taking Communion; and even later, when they began to gather in monasteries, their chief concern was still with conduct rather than the sacraments. They went ravening after perfection, forsaking the world and its vaunts, denying the desires of the flesh, laboring at the meanest tasks, wearing the foulest clothes, eating little, sleeping brokenly, and praying hour after hour. They were, to use William James's language, "sick souls"—but the race itself was sick. The world was in ruins, and life was a feeble and wounded thing crawling about amid the wreckage. No wonder then that these, the flower of the race, the noblest and bravest and most learned of the day, could only cry: "We speak as dying men to dying men: repent while there is yet time!"

Had monasticism remained sporadic and unorganized, it might have spent itself before long and disappeared. What saved it—and ultimately destroyed it—was the order which crept into it and changed it from a scattered rout to a steady movement. As early as the beginning of the fifth century the Eastern monasteries began to accept the "Rule of St. Basil" which fixed a routine for their inmates. Western monasticism took longer to regulate, largely because of the greater chaos in the region. Until the middle of the sixth century, each establishment had its own rule which usually was influenced by the local environment. For instance in Ireland, which was inhabited by tribes traditionally addicted to fighting, the monasteries were largely armed camps which terrorized the countryside and sometimes made forays even against each other.

St. Benedict

But gradually this anarchy disappeared and the abuses and laxities were suppressed. The man chiefly responsible for the reform was St. Benedict, who about 529 founded a great monastery on Monte Cassino, in Italy. Possessing both Christian piety and a Roman genius for organization, he drew up a "rule" which became in time even more widely accepted in the West than was St. Basil's in the East. Benedict insisted that each monastery should be a permanent, self-contained, and self-supporting garrison of Christ's soldiers. A monk was not free to wander about from one establishment to another. Once he had served his year of trial and was established in a "house," he was bound by vows to remain there till he died. His cloister had to be the whole world to him thenceforth, and its inmates his entire society.

The common life of the brethren was subsumed under three heads: Prayer, Labor, and Self-denial. At least four hours of each day had to be spent in worship, and the periods, seven in number, were fixed with precision. The aim was to fulfill the words of the 119th psalm: "In the midst of the night I will rise up to give thanks unto Thee . . . seven times a day do I praise Thee." Accordingly the monks were commanded to rise up at midnight for Matins and Lauds, which were practically one service. At six in the morning came the second service, Prime, and then at three-hour intervals came Tierce, Sext, and None. The sixth service, Vespers, was chanted shortly after sundown, and the seventh, Compline, came after a short public reading from the *Collationes* of St. Cassian. Each service, as a rule, consisted of three psalms and a little additional matter, and therefore took from twenty minutes to half an hour. But besides these there was to be considerable private prayer.

Labor and Self-Denial

Even more time, however, was to be given to labor, for, as the wise Benedict declared, "idleness is the enemy of the soul." Usually this work was in the fields and vineyards, since enough food and drink had to be produced by the monastery to provide for the wants of all its inmates. And a portion of each day had to be devoted to reading, for ignorance like idleness was frowned upon by Benedict. The monks were to assemble in the cloister, which, though covered in, was open to the weather, and there they were to pore over their scrolls. Those who were skilled with the pen were assigned to copy manuscripts, for each monastery had to have a library. And such as were well versed in letters, and had good voices, might read to those who were near of sight or illiterate. Benedict did not expect the monks to be scholars. He himself was no scholar, as is evident from his colloquial Latin, and from his biographer's comment that he was "knowingly ignorant and wisely unlearned." All he demanded was that the mind as well as the body be occupied.

The self-denial ordained for the brethren was relatively moderate. There were three vows to be taken, Poverty, Obedience, and Chastity, and from at least the last two not even the Pope could grant a dispensation. Poverty was to be absolute in the personal sense— though the corporation was allowed to own all it could legitimately lay hold of. But there was to be no private property whatsoever, and the abbot was instructed to make frequent search in the corners, and even in the monks' mattresses, for hidden hoards. If a brother was found guilty of hiding possessions, he might be buried alive in the middle of the convent dunghill!

Other Rules

Obedience, too, was to be absolute. The monk must be utterly subservient to his abbot, who stood in the place of Christ, and must obey implicitly without ever asking why. And the practice of Chastity, the third of the vows, was, of course, taken for granted.

Beside these *tria substantialia*, there were certain minor prescriptions. Food and drink were to be reduced to an endurable minimum, but no further. Only the sick were permitted the meat of animals, but the rest might on occasion eat poultry. Bread, vegetables, and fish— which was counted the least defiling of fleshly foods because it was imagined to be produced without copulation—were the staples of diet. And a daily allowance of a hemina—about half a pint—of wine was permitted to each monk. Silence was to be absolute during most of the day, and there was to be no buffoonery or laughter. Warm baths were a rare concession; cold ones were never taken even as a penance. Finally there was to be frequent resort to corporal punishment even for the slightest infractions.

Value of Benedict's Rule

Such in brief was Benedict's Rule, and its sanity and practicability soon commended it to earnest men throughout the West. It established a mode of life immensely desirable in that age. Europe was still a wasteland swarming with marauding tribes and robber bands. Might was the only law, and he who was not attached to some feudal chieftain was lost. In the monastery, however, a man was safe. Once enrolled as a monk, the round of daily tasks was established beyond change, and all life became ordered and plain. One ceased to be a man among men; one became a sworn soldier of Christ.

By the time of Charlemagne, in the ninth century, the whole of the West was dotted with these garrisons of Christ's soldiers, and through them a new spirit was brought into the life of Christendom. There was never an "order" of Benedictines; each "house" was autonomous and self-contained. Yet all were bound together by a common routine, and the monks formed as it were one cohesive army. They spread out everywhere, setting up religious blockhouses in the midst of the newly conquered lands to hold them fast to what came to be called the Holy Roman Empire. They became the chief instruments in the conversion of the Barbarians, and in the reformation of the Christians themselves.

Most important of all, the monks became the conservers of what little learning still survived in the West. From the time of Cassiodorus, a contemporary of Benedict whom some historians consider of even greater significance, the cowled men labored to save for posterity the divine and human knowledge which the tide of barbarism threatened to obliterate completely. If their success was limited, it was solely because the task was too severe. By the time the monks came to see that it was their duty to save the world's culture as well as their own souls, the process of decay was already too far gone. What "profane" manuscripts the earlier Christians had failed to burn in their campaigns against Paganism, were largely destroyed or mislaid during the Barbarian invasions. Very little save the Holy Writ and the writings of the Church Fathers was left in the West, and even that little was in a tragically garbled form. Greek and Hebrew were hardly known, and even classic Latin was rapidly becoming a forgotten tongue. The populace spoke the jargons of the Barbarian races, or, in Italy itself, a vernacular Latin lacking grammar and literature. Even so great a monarch as Charlemagne could hardly read or write. Most of the lesser priests were able to serve at the altars only because they knew the prayers by rote.

In a world so dark the wonder is not that the monks accomplished little, but that they accomplished anything at all. For aside from them, and a rare king like Charlemagne or Alfred the Great, there were none who gave a thought to learning. The monks alone conducted what few schools were to be found in Europe in the Dark Ages. They alone preserved the ancient manuscripts and copied them. They alone wrote commentaries on the Scriptures and on the surviving fragments of Plato and Aristotle. They alone kept chronicles, compiled texts, and stared at earth and sky with inquiring eyes. One pictures the monasteries as so many tiny candle flames glimmering fitfully in the blackness of the night. Here they were clustered thickly, and there scattered wide; in Italy, France, and the British Isles they seemed actually to have flared for a time, but in the northern forests and on the Eastern steppes they were barely able to gutter. Yet everywhere they kept burning—the last embers of a glory that had once illumined the earth, and the first of a greater glory to come.

The Crusades Produce Many Long-Lasting Effects

by Jonathan Riley-Smith

The Holy Land had been conquered by Arab Muslims in the A.D. 600s. They allowed Christians to visit the sacred sites there, but during the eleventh century fierce Seljuk Turks from Asia took control of the Holy Land and interfered with Christian pilgrims. As a result, in 1095 Pope Urban II, after a plea for help from the Byzantine emperor Alexius Comnenus, urged Christians to rescue the Holy Land from the Turks. Christians had already taken back land seized by earlier Muslim attacks in Italy, Sicily, and Spain, so this appeal was enthusiastically received. Several Crusades followed, but the end result was failure to hold on to Christian gains in the Holy Land. However, these military expeditions did expose Westerners to Byzantine and Islamic cultures, increased their interest in trade and travel, and spurred improvements in military tactics and weapons. In the following interview, Jonathan Riley-Smith, professor of history at Royal Holloway and Bedford New College (University of London), explains other long-lasting effects of the Crusades.

Christian History: In the first three centuries, Christians were pacifists. By 1096, they embarked on a holy war. What caused such a huge change?

Jonathan Riley-Smith: First, the early church was not entirely pacifist. In Romans 13, for example, Paul justifies the violence of the pagan emperor, for the emperor is yet a minister of God. And Christians served in the Roman army from the second century on.

Following the conversion of the emperors, in the fourth century, the church became more open to using violence. Church leaders, after an initial shock, began supporting the use of force against heretics.

Then Augustine formulated his theory of "just war," but his terms effectively mean "holy war." Augustine and the medieval world concluded that violence is not evil. Instead, violence is morally neutral. That makes a crusade possible.

How did medieval Christians support their idea that violence was morally neutral?

Augustine gave this example: Suppose a man has gangrene in the leg and is going to die. The surgeon believes the only way to save him is by amputating the leg. Against the man's will, the surgeon straps him to a table and saws off the leg. That is an act of extreme violence.

But was that violence evil? Augustine said no. And if you find one exception to the idea that violence is evil, he concluded, then violence cannot be intrinsically evil.

Thus, for medieval theologians, violence may or may not be evil; it depends largely on the intention of the perpetrator. Until the sixteenth and seventeenth centuries, this was the normative Christian view. In fact, the majority of Christians over 2,000 years have believed that violence may be justified under certain circumstances.

It's one thing to say violence is morally neutral, but how did the crusaders justify an offensive strike against Islam?

If you had asked a canon lawyer (theologian), he would have said the Crusades were *defensive:* Christians were defending their brothers and sisters in the East from Muslim aggression and oppression, or they were regaining land that had been taken by Muslims. Senior churchmen maintained that when Christianity goes to war, it can only be in defense or for the recovery of property.

But if you had mingled with a crowd of knights in the late eleventh century, they would have said they were fighting for "the liberation of Jerusalem." That's not so hard to understand when you consider that Christians reach the same conclusions today.

Christians crusade today?

Think about the more militant advocates of Christian liberation. Although liberationists argue for rebellion rather than war, they put forward arguments that were made in the twelfth and thirteenth centuries: Violence is morally neutral; Christ intends people to live in just political structures; Christ is present in the process of liberation; we must show solidarity with our oppressed brothers and sisters; dying in this cause is martyrdom.

It's often said that Christians were more cruel than the Muslims—for example, when they captured a city. Do you think that's true?

I don't think it is. The case that is always given is this: When the Christians took Jerusalem in 1099, they mercilessly sacked the city, killing nearly everyone; but when the Muslims under Saladin captured Jerusalem in 1187, they allowed captives to go free.

But that example accords with the medieval laws of war: if a city surrenders, you don't sack it; if it resists, you do. Jerusalem resisted in 1099, and it was sacked. When it surrendered in 1187, it was not. In actuality, you find cruelty on both sides.

We must also be aware of combat psychology. Long campaigns, as many of the Crusades were, put tremendous stress on combatants. Today we recognize that under the stress of battle and fatigue, discipline can disintegrate, often with tragic consequences.

In the late nineteenth century, people looked at the crusaders and said, "These are brutal men." Modern historians are likely to add, "These are also brutalized men."

Yet how can we understand the slaughtering of entire villages of Jews in Germany? This happened at the very beginning of a campaign.

In this area, the Christians behaved abominably. Too often, Christians have excused these horrendous persecutions on the grounds that they were led by peasants and rabble. That is not strictly true; the so-called People's Crusade was led by a significant number of nobles and knights. We have to face up to the terrible crimes committed by these Christians.

Why did they do it? Remember that in order to sell the crusading idea to the masses, preachers had to use ideas that people understood. And they used terms of family: "The Eastern Christians are your brothers and sisters, and they are being persecuted by the Muslims. Christ is your Father, and he has been shamed, because his estate has been taken away by the Muslims. You must go to defend your brothers and sisters and to recover your Father's patrimony!"

This was the great age of the vendetta, and knights and nobles immediately thought in terms of blood feud and revenge. They responded to this preaching: "We are called upon to avenge the occupation of our Father's land in 638 [when Muslims occupied the Holy Land]."

But soon they added, "What about the destruction of his body in 33? Why shouldn't we punish these people who have disparaged our Father's honor even more than the Muslims did?"

Church leaders tried to halt that line of reasoning, but once they had taken the cork out of the bottle, they could not put it back in.

How much did greed for land or riches motivate crusaders?

Very little, because most crusaders became poorer as a result of their crusades.

A German knight called to fight in Italy in the mid-twelfth century, for example, expected his expenses to be twice his annual salary. If we assume that to live like a knight now would require $50,000 a year, that means his expenses were $100,000. A French or English knight crusading to the Holy Land might spend twice as much! The only way to raise this much money was to sell property.

Neither did crusaders get rich from booty. They did bring home relics, but you cannot sell relics; canon law forbids it. I know of no case of a crusader returning home rich.

We picture people, without a thought in the world, galloping off to the East. But we have to remember how unpleasant crusades were. Medieval Christians were frightened by them. Would you want to walk 2,000 miles, starve yourself periodically, drink only the dirtiest water, and subject yourself to violence?

How many people did, in fact, venture forth to crusade? And how many died as a result?

Throughout the crusading period, only a minority of people actually went on a crusade. The First Crusade was organized when there were probably 50,000 nobles and knights in France alone, yet only about 5,000 of these went.

As far as those who died, we simply don't have accurate information. Thousands and thousands, certainly. But from the medieval perspective, death is beside the point. Humbert of Romans, a great Crusades preacher, said, "The aim of Christianity is not to fill the earth, but to fill heaven."

What happened to the crusading ideal once Christians were expelled from the Holy Land in 1291?

The traditional date, 1291, is convenient for marking the end of the Crusades for Jerusalem. But 1291 is no longer a significant date to crusades historians.

There are as many crusades going on in the fourteenth century as there were in the thirteenth—some against Muslims, and some against heretics. Even as late as 1580 you have a crusade to Morocco that fits all the features of crusading.

We think of the Crusades as a military and political failure. Is that true?

In the Holy Land, they did fail. But the larger crusading movement was successful in preserving Christian Europe. Europe was threatened by Islam. For example, Muslims were advancing from the late fourteenth century to the late seventeenth century. Vienna, in the heart of Europe, was besieged twice—once in 1683, which is not very long ago. People were terrified of being invaded.

What would have happened in Spain, the Balkans, and in northern Europe without the various Crusades against Muslims? The Muslims would have advanced, and the history of Europe and of Christianity would have been entirely different.

What were some of the unintended results of crusading?
One was a great advance in the field of nursing.

At the time, surgery was extremely limited. But the Salerno school of medicine taught that you should keep patients warm, clean, and quiet. This method was adopted by a crusader military order, the Hospitallers of St. John, and because of their influence, it spread throughout Western Europe.

The Crusades also introduced the income tax, without which no modern government could finance itself.

Did crusades bring any benefit to the church, to the average Christian?

The Crusades also developed the use of indulgences. For Protestants, this is a sticky affair, because they see how the indulgence was later corrupted. But for Catholics, the fully developed indulgence was a great advance in pastoral care.

Medieval men and women, especially in the twelfth and thirteenth centuries, were obsessed with their sinfulness. They felt themselves locked in a world of sin, a world from which there was only one escape: renouncing the world entirely and going into a religious community.

Penance was available, of course, but one had to pay back to God an equivalent of the sin committed. Medieval Christians instinctively knew nothing they could do—crawling on their knees to Rome, standing in a stream for six months, whatever—could compensate for sin.

The indulgence simply said, "Such is God's mercy, that he will treat your penitent act as though it were satisfactory (even though it is not)." Indulgences were an application of God's love and mercy and grace to an uneasy conscience.

With an indulgence to go on a crusade, people didn't have to enter the monastery. By traveling or soldiering, they could get on their way to heaven.

This yearning for salvation sounds like the spiritual unrest just prior to the Protestant Reformation.

It is very similar. The Crusades come during the eleventh-century reformation.

In Europe today, if you drive five miles along any road, you will probably find two churches. Nearly all of those churches are built on eleventh- and twelfth-century foundations. Previously, there might have been one church every twenty miles, from which priests would go out to serve the sacraments. Eleventh-century reformers believed religion should be taken into the villages, and this evangelizing drive resulted in a great building program. This burst of construction ranks with anything the Roman Empire did. Someone in 1032 said, "France is becoming white with churches."

Now, as one historian has pointed out, every Christian reformation is accompanied by violence—take for example, the Protestant Reformation, which led into the wars of religion. The eleventh-century reformation was no exception.

Are the Crusades a root of the problems in the Middle East today between Christians, Jews, and Arabs?

They might have contributed to the problem. If you talk to Arabs now, they express bitter feelings about crusading.

Ironically, the Arabs actually won the Holy Land Crusades. Christians as a political and military force were driven out in 1291 and haven't returned since.

What should we think of crusaders?

First, we need to understand that medieval crusaders are likely to be our relatives. If you are of Western European origin, you have nearly a 100-percent chance of being a direct descendant of someone who had a link with a crusade. Even if your ancestors did not go on a crusade, they would have paid taxes to finance crusades, and they would have attended crusade sermons.

Second, as a historian I try to understand what people did and why they did it. Why did medieval Christians risk their lives and sacrifice nearly all they owned to crusade? Given the historical setting and their understanding, were these people trying to express love of God and neighbor through crusading? Though I cannot condone all of their actions, I have to say they were.

Gutenberg's Bible Catalyzes the Protestant Reformation

by John Man

Human communication has taken three huge historical leaps, all due to important inventions. The first was writing, the second was the alphabet, and the third was the movable-type printing press, invented by Johannes Gutenberg of Mainz, Germany, in the early 1450s. Before Gutenberg's time, though literacy and the demand for books had increased dramatically in Europe, the traditional method of producing books, hand copying by scribes, made books prohibitively expensive and limited their availability to common people. By 1452 Gutenberg had begun producing the first printed book, a Latin translation of the Bible, a task he considered his life's goal. By 1456 he had completed his task.

The following excerpt, by John Man, a historian and author with a background in German studies and the history of science, explains the immediate and cumulative effects of Gutenberg's printed Bible, from its rapid and inexpensive distribution among the European population to its role in the dissident movement of Martin Luther against excesses and corruption in the Catholic Church.

In Victor Hugo's *Notre-Dame de Paris*, a scholar gazes at the first printed book to come his way and stares out at the cathedral, an encyclopedia in stone and statuary and stained glass recording Christian faith and knowledge passed on from generation to generation. *'Ceci tuera cela,'* he says: 'This will kill that', the printed word will bring an end to stories in stone, and—the words imply— to received religion as passed on by priests and their artists. Hugo, speaking with the advantage of hindsight, was distilling into three words a process of fragmentation that, although under way since before Gutenberg's time, was made irreversible by the printed word.

Initial Church Reaction

The Church at first welcomed the power of the press as a gift of God when it was used to raise cash for a crusade against the Turks. Its blessings seemed somewhat mixed when used by opposing sides in Mainz's civil war. But the true power of what had been unleashed became apparent only in the beginnings of the vast and permanent change in European history that came to be called the Reformation. As with printing, the elements were all present—anticlericalism, corruption, the non-religious philosophies of humanism, a desire for change, resurgent nationalism, a hatred of Roman domination—lacking only a focus and a flashpoint. Wittenberg, a small town in Saxony, was the tinderbox, and Martin Luther the match.

It's a story often told, but, like Gutenberg's, there is still a mystery at its heart. It repays a close look, because these events reveal again the explosive power released when character, circumstances and technology collide. We are about to see a gear shift in the engine of revolution started by Gutenberg. . . .

What happened next has been the subject of a huge debate. Traditionally, on the eve of All Saints' Day, 31 October 1517, Luther took his ninety-five 'theses' [a condemnation of church practices such as the sale of indulgences, or remission of sins] and nailed them to the door of Wittenberg's castle church, so that those entering that morning to view the relics put on show for the feast day would see them. [Though the story is almost certainly a legend] it is a powerful image, a man hammering on a church door, driving a nail into the coffin of Catholic corruption. It was, we were told, the way one announced an academic debate. Then, suddenly, it was out of his hands. Someone copied the theses, and they were printed and flew all over Germany, leaving no one more surprised than Luther. It is a story now embedded in history books, and recalled on Wittenberg's church doors today; not the original wooden doors, which were damaged by fire in the nineteenth century, but their bronze replacements, across which the theses run in six columns. . . .

The Spread of Luther's Ideas

At this moment events leaped out of control. Somehow, as is the way with sensitive documents, the theses got out. Possibly, the source was one of the experts in Mainz, though it seems unlikely that any local printer . . . would risk [archbishop of Mainz] Albrecht's anger by publishing without permission. There are other possibilities. Luther had sent copies to a few other trusted friends, among them his immediate superior, Jerome Scultetus (Hieronymus Schultze), the bishop of Brandenburg. In any event, by mid-December enough people knew for security to be compromised. Someone, no one knows who, leaked the theses, and the dam broke with astonishing speed.

Later, Luther would claim that it was all over Germany in two weeks. Not quite; but just before Christmas—virtually the same day that Albrecht received the advice of his Mainz experts—editions of the theses, translated into German, appeared in Leipzig, Basel, Nuremberg and (almost certainly) Wittenberg itself. As suddenly, as fame comes to pop singers and football superstars today, Luther was a household name and everyone was talking about his devastating theses. The indulgences market collapsed like a popped dot com.

The noises that accompanied Luther's message of doom were probably not hammer-blows; they were the squeaks and bangs of busy printing presses. . . .

Johannes Gutenberg's invention of the movable-type printing press made the Bible accessible to common people throughout Europe.

As Rome prepared its heavy artillery, Luther fired off more salvos, with the help of the press. His sermons, tracts and polemics, all in German the better to appeal to his audience, streamed from presses by the hundreds of thousands across the land, many with his portrait (some 700 of these *Flugschriften*—'flying writings'—have survived). He became the focus of a propaganda war of which Mainz in 1460–62 had been a tiny precedent, and a publishing phenomenon, unrivalled anywhere, ever, except perhaps by Mao's *Little Red Book* at the height of China's Cultural Revolution. At least two of Luther's sermons ran through twenty editions in two or three years. According to one estimate, a third of all books printed in Germany between 1518 and 1525 were by him. Pause to consider that figure. Of course, printing was in its infancy, but Germany at the time was turning out about a million books a year, of which a third—300,000—were by Luther. No comparison with the modern world stands up, but it would be the equivalent of one author selling almost 300 million books in Britain (which prints some 800 million a year), or 700 million in the US, every year, for seven years running.

Of his thunderous outpourings, perhaps the most powerful was his *Address to the Christian Nobility of the German Nation*, a sort of Reformation manifesto. His conclusion, in German of course, was virtually a call to arms. Every Christian leader had a duty to reform the Church: 'Whoever is guilty should suffer,' he said, and then in a righteous fury: 'Listen to this, Pope, not the all-holiest but the all, most-sinful, let God right now destroy thy seat!' Its first run was in the shops on 18 August. Within days it was sold out, to be reprinted a week later. In three weeks it sold 4,000 copies—in Wittenberg alone, where the printers became rich. In the next two years it went through thirteen editions, with pirated versions appearing in Leipzig, Strasbourg and Basel. German princes heard and took note. . . .

In this story, a dominant theme is the emergence of a new national sentiment. Luther addressed the 'German nation' in its own language; his appeal was to a people fed up with foreign domination; his robust language founded a cultural nationalism with dramatic and enduring political impact, though it would take four centuries to work to its logical conclusion, the creation of a nation-state. But the forces unleashed in Germany—press, language, nationalism—applied everywhere in Europe. . . .

Few doubted how much these momentous changes owed to the power of the press. Gutenberg, once the darling of the Catholics, now became a Protestant hero. Printing, Luther said, was 'God's highest and extremest act of grace, whereby the business of the Gospel is driven forward', freeing Germany from the shackles of Rome, and his followers agreed. Johann Sleidan, historian, wrote in 1542: 'As if to offer proof that God has chosen to accomplish a special mission, there was invented in our land a marvellous new and subtle art, the art of printing. This opened Germany's eyes, even as it is now bringing enlightenment to other countries.' A popular metaphor, echoed in many Reformation publications, compared the printing press to its forerunner, the wine press, from which poured a new and noble vintage. As John Foxe put it in his *Book of Martyrs* (1563): 'The Lord began to work for His Church not with sword and target to subdue His exalted adversary, but with printing, writing and reading. . . . Either the Pope must abolish knowledge and printing or printing must at length root him out.'

The Catholic Church Fights Back

The papacy, of course, had no intention of being rooted out, and fought back, using the same 'divine art', as Nicholas of Cusa [a cardinal of the Catholic Church] had called it. In a sense, Nicholas of Cusa and Gutenberg achieved their aim in part, in that it was now possible to produce uniform texts throughout the Catholic world. But since that world was now under threat, uniformity turned into something that was rather less of a virtue—a severe conservatism, denying change. Certain ideas that were once merely up for discussion, like Aristotelian cosmology, became fixed. Rule books on how to define sin and how sermons were to be preached issued from Rome's stern presses.

It was not enough. If some works needed to be published, others certainly didn't—a view that inspired the response that has won the Church its most scathing condemnation from non-Catholics: its attempt to control the press by banning those works of which it disapproved.

The Church had always claimed the right to approve or disapprove of books, and there had been occasional bannings, easy to impose by the Inquisition when monks produced the books for other monks. But the advent of printing raised the stakes, and the coming of the Reformation raised them higher still. In 1542, Pope Paul III set up a local branch of the Inquisition, as opposed to its fearsome Spanish counterpart, to counteract the Reformation, which it did by initiating a reign of terror that Spanish inquisitors must have envied. One of its functions was to condemn heretical books, a task paralleled in France by the Sorbonne, which published its own list of banned books. The Council of Trent (1545–63), called to retrench after the Protestant defection, established a centralised list of books that existed thanks to that *accursed* invention, printing—a list that, thanks to that *divine* invention, printing, could be distributed across the world of the faithful. Published first in 1559, the list grew year by year, and so did its malign reputation.

Actually, it was not all malign, because the *Index Librorum Prohibitorum* proclaimed what was new and interesting, and acted as good advertising for Protestant publishers. Banning never really worked: in France the official bookseller Jean André printed both the *Index* and the work of the banned heretic poet Clément Marot. Being banned was a sort of recommendation. Those on the *Index* in the early days included Peter Abelard, Lefèvre d'Etaples (the first translator of the Bible into French), Boccaccio, Calvin, Dante, Erasmus, Rabelais and, of course, Luther. Eventually, there would be 4,000 books on the *Index* by the time it was disbanded in 1966.

It's easy to carp. It is the fate of censors worldwide to be reviled and ridiculed. But since the *Index* was a notorious failure—its banned authors included Voltaire, Rousseau, Gibbon, Balzac, Flaubert, Descartes and Darwin—perhaps it should not be condemned with quite the severity that should be reserved for successful censorships, of which the last century has seen a few. In its favour, as Norman Davies points out in *Europe: A History*, the Vatican saw nothing subversive about Milton's *Eikonoklastes* (banned in England in 1660) or even *Lady Chatterley's Lover* (banned in Britain from 1928 to 1960). Its inconsistencies and inadequacies seem now an admission that it was too late to do anything much about a medium that was beyond control.

CHAPTER 3

The Reformation and Beyond (1517–Present)

Luther Breaks with Traditional Christianity

by Martin E. Marty

The Catholic Church was awash in scandal in the early 1500s. The church had been granting indulgences (forgiving punishment for sins) in exchange for money. The large amount of money gained by this endeavor reflected badly on the church. Into this corruption came a man who wanted to change it.

Martin Luther became a priest in 1507 and was appointed professor of theology at the University of Wittenberg in 1512. Though he held a respected position, he struggled with an overpowering sense of his own sinfulness. No matter what he did, Luther felt that sin held sway over him. Luther made an important discovery about God's justice as he prepared his lectures in 1515. How could anyone find favor with a holy God? Luther believed no person could be good enough for God. Instead, faith in Christ saves humans from God's repugnance at their sins. This revelation caused him to become incensed over the church's insistence that sins could be forgiven only if people adhered to the church's rules. The legendary story is that to protest the church's practices, Luther nailed his famous Ninety-five Theses on to the Wittenburg church door. Due to the invention of the movable-type printing press, his written message soon spread across Europe, igniting a revolution against entrenched church practices.

Martin E. Marty, a historian, writer, and professor at the University of Chicago, discusses in the following interview both intended and unintended consequences of Luther's revolution.

Christian History: If Luther were alive today, what would he be writing theses about?

Martin Marty: Every historian says we can't answer that kind of question, and then every historian answers it!

We have to remember that every historical figure is, in one sense, inaccessible to the modern world. Historian Heiko Oberman reminds us that Luther lived in a different world—a world of witches and unstoppable plagues. So it's not easy to grab somebody out of his or her context.

That said, we can have some fun hazarding guesses. There's no more consistent strand in Luther from 1513 [when he begins lecturing on the Bible] to 1546 [when he dies] than the gospel of forgiveness. That theme still isn't heeded well.

In our day, we emphasize the gospel of self-esteem, marketing the church based on people's needs, saying, "I found it!" and "I'm the little engine that could." Our culture promotes human ability and human will, as did the indulgence culture in Luther's day, as a way to bring salvation. So I have a hunch Luther would still feel compelled to speak his central message.

Would Luther quarrel with Roman Catholicism today?

The language of the sacrifice of the Mass, which disturbed Luther more than anything else, still remains. Yet there's a hint of a whisper that today's Catholic understanding isn't that much different from what we mean in most Protestant Communion services when we talk about offering ourselves in response to the Lord. Within Catholicism today, there is less accent on the Mass being a priestly act of good works.

Also, when I look at Catholic teachings on the Book of Romans and the Book of Galatians, most of which acknowledge the critical role of grace and faith, I have to say Luther has made his point. I don't know that he would be as disturbed with Catholicism today as he was in the 1500s.

At the Second Vatican Council, in our lifetime, the Roman Catholic church profoundly reshaped itself. If those changes had come at the Council of Trent, in Luther's lifetime, would there still be one church in the West?

No. There isn't ever going to be one church in the West. However much I may yearn for such unity, I don't believe it's possible in the modern world—a world of choice, diversity, rapid communication, and human autonomy. In the face of the many, many cultures in today's world, I have no way of picturing something called the Western Church.

Is there any place, then, for Protestant-Catholic dialogue?

I think the most important Protestant-Catholic dialogue is what happens in Decatur, Illinois, and Dover, Delaware. It happens when people work in homeless shelters or do joint Bible studies or canvas their neighborhoods or jointly sponsor refugees. It happens when Catholic and Protestant seminaries offer cooperative courses. That's when real dialogue occurs.

Where do you most see Luther's impact on our world?

I don't believe in the heroic concept of history, in

which one person overshadows everything. I see Luther in the context of late medieval ferment: there is reform all over, and somehow a revolt in the junior faculty at Wittenberg is the one that catches on. Because Luther is a titanic character, he leaves his stamp on history.

In history, when there was a ferment of drama, out of it came Shakespeare. When there was an emphasis on the epic, out of it came Homer. When there was a stirring of democratic idealism, Jefferson emerged. Luther is one of those figures who summarizes an age.

Having said that, I have a hard time picturing several aspects of the modern world without Luther. Take, for example, the prominence of the gospel of forgiveness. Though others championed this doctrine as well, Luther was fiery hot. That emphasis (though maybe not with the same heat) still characterizes half a billion people called Anglican, Lutheran, Baptist, Evangelical, and the like. That is the longest shadow Luther casts today.

Also, Luther stands symbolically as the greatest single agent in increasing the value of the individual. What eventually emerges (although it took two more centuries and couldn't have happened without the Enlightenment) is a new kind of individual. That made democratic government possible.

What forces, if any, did Luther not intend to set in motion?

Luther would never have said he contributed to modern nationalism. Particularly in his later writings you find endless heapings on the German people: he saw them as loutish, selfish, drunk, self-centered, stupid.

Still, Luther politically and culturally coalesced the German people; he helped to unite in language and culture the two hundred to three hundred little Germanic states. Luther thus contributed to the breaking up of the Holy Roman Empire and the rise of nationalism.

Nationalism, of course, is a mixed blessing. We're better off with it than we were with the Holy Roman Empire or with tribalism. But modern nationalism is often the rival of the Christian faith; it summons almost idolatrous assent. And Luther inadvertently contributed to this force.

Martin Luther sparked the Protestant Reformation when he issued his Ninety-five Theses detailing corruption within the Catholic Church.

Second, Luther contributed to anti-Semitism in Germany. Because Jews frustrated him by not accepting the gospel, he turned on them, writing, "Burn their synagogues and drive them out!" Not much happened with that sentiment for a couple of centuries, but beginning in the 1800s, anti-Semitism increased more and more. It's stupid to say Luther is Hitler's spiritual ancestor. But it's not stupid to say that in his rather blind striking out at Jews, Luther unintentionally provided the passion, vocabulary, and rationale for some horrible things that happened to Jews in our time.

Any positive, though unintended, legacies of Luther?

Luther contributed unintentionally to the rising status of women.

He was patriarchal, but I teach my students to judge people in the context of their time, and for his day, Luther was progressive. He assumed that girls, along with boys, should be taught the catechism, and in that he anticipated co-education. He insisted that marriage was just as important a vocation as monasticism, and in that he accorded greater status to a woman's role in marriage. And he was married to and proud of a woman who was, in effect, the treasurer, manager, and administrator of a rather complex business—the informal boarding house that the Luthers kept.

From Luther's day to ours, people have suggested the great reformer was somehow psychologically troubled. Is there any basis to those charges?

Luther often showed signs of being troubled, and at times he himself all but said that. But my hunch is that all geniuses are psychologically troubled in one way or another. Mozart, Michelangelo, Goethe, Dante, Milton —almost every creative genius except Bach—seemed somehow to be a misfit in the world. That leads such people to set the world right, and it leads them to create great works of beauty or agony. People who live in complete serenity with the world, who are completely balanced, make wonderful citizens and good Christians, but they probably don't leave works of genius behind them.

Is Luther a model for you?

Yes. First, in music. In the Protestant churches, we take for granted our singing tradition. We forget that singing used to belong only to monks and priests. But as a result of Luther, lay people erupt in song, and composers are inspired.

I never go through a day without listening to some Lutheran chorales or organ renditions of great Christian music. Luther wrote that music is next to theology, and I'm convinced he liked music better than theology.

Second, I get a great deal out of Luther's concept of vocation. I believe that if people could see the connection between the gospel of forgiveness and vocation, guilt and worry would be minimized. It's a message that each day is a new start: you're not held back by what has been, and you're not haunted by the future. I would like to see a therapy built on this great concept.

Third, Luther reminds me that one does not try to attain access to God on God's level, but on the human level. I'm not interested in contemplation or meditation or seeing the face of God directly. In the Heidelberg Disputation, Luther said we have to be content with the hind parts of God.

Consequently, I look to God as he has made himself plainly visible to us in the sacrifice of Christ, in the Bible, in the church, and in divine actions in history. Naturally, this inspires me very much as a historian.

Thomas Cranmer Helps Henry VIII Break with Rome and Begin the English Reformation

by Alister McGrath

Henry VIII came to power in England in 1509 with political and religious strife on the horizon. When Martin Luther posted his theses in 1517, Henry wrote a book that attacked the German priest, thus gaining approval of the pope in Rome. But the English people did not support Henry; the church corruption and immorality Luther preached against were evident in England too. Scholars and theologians in England called for reform at the same time. Nationalistic feelings developed, as they had elsewhere across Europe, and Henry seized the opportunity to break with Rome, afforded by his clash with the pope over the king's multiple marriages and divorces.

Henry depended on Thomas Cranmer, a Cambridge scholar with Lutheran leanings, for advice in this confrontation. Eventually the king appointed Cranmer archbishop of Canterbury to give legitimacy to his strife with Rome. In 1534 Parliament legalized the break with Rome, Henry declared himself head of the new Church of England, and the Catholic Church's political supremacy was over.

Alister McGrath, "The Christian History Interview: The Tradition Continues," *Christian History*, 1997. Copyright © 1997 by Alister McGrath. Reproduced by permission.

In the following interview, Alister McGrath, professor of theology at Oxford University and author of many books, explores Cranmer's role in establishing the Church of England, or Anglican Church. In particular, he discusses Cranmer's valuable contribution—the Book of Common Prayer.

———————————

Christian History: If Cranmer hadn't lived, or if he had been martyred earlier [Cranmer was burned at the stake in 1556, on the order of Henry's Catholic daughter and successor, Mary], how might the English Reformation have been different?

Alister McGrath: It may have taken longer to achieve. Cranmer was a diplomat. He was prepared to give Henry what he wanted while he tried to accomplish his Reformation agenda. Sometimes he did things against his own will—like enforcing Henry's Six Articles, especially the article requiring priestly celibacy. But Cranmer realized that if he didn't go along, the Reformation wouldn't continue.

In Henry's reign, people in high positions tended to have short lives because Henry was determined to get his way. Cranmer managed to stay alive and made at least some headway for the Reformation.

Having survived Henry's reign, Cranmer was in a position to push the Reformation forward much more speedily under Edward VI. That, in fact, is when he made his greatest contributions, the *Book of Common Prayer* and the Forty-Two Articles.

Considering he recanted several times, how much impact did his martyrdom have?

It excited a lot of reaction. Some scholars argue that

the popular rise against Queen Mary was partly due to his dramatic recantation of his recantations, and of his holding forth his right hand into the fire. [Cranmer withdrew his final letter of submission to the pope, and in a famous scene at his execution, declared that he died a Protestant and held his right hand in the fire till it burned to a stump, as penance for the sin of writing a lie with that hand.]

Clearly the recantations were a problem. Cranmer was a fallible and weak man, yet he showed strength when strength really needed to be shown. Consequently, in his death, Cranmer may have had as great an influence as he had in his life.

Is Cranmer a household name in England today?

No. The English Reformation has no major name associated with it. It was pushed forward by a collection of people, and none of them are in the same league as Luther or Calvin.

Of the English Reformers, Cranmer would probably be the most familiar. But most English people tend to remember Cranmer either for his *Book of Common Prayer* or for his martyrdom. But I don't think there's any great popular understanding of what Cranmer stood for theologically.

What is distinctive about the Anglican Christianity Cranmer and others carved out?

First, like the Reformation in general, it puts a major emphasis on Scripture and the importance of doctrines such as justification by faith.

But this is supplemented by a strong emphasis on historical continuity. Tradition mattered to Cranmer, and he was particularly interested in patristics, the writings of the early church fathers. To Anglicans, the early church is seen as a defining moment in the interpretation of Scripture. Therefore, writers like Augustine, Athanasius, and others are of major importance.

That carries through to this day. If you look at the writings of Anglican evangelicals like James Packer and John Stott, they constantly refer to those who have interpreted Scripture before us.

Obviously one Anglican distinctive would be the use of the Book of Common Prayer.

For Anglicans, having a set public liturgy is extremely important. Liturgy does many things, one of which is to encourage doctrinal correctness. The words of the liturgy embody an orthodox Christianity, so that a priest or parishioner who is theologically unorthodox is still required to use an orthodox liturgy.

A public liturgy also keeps in check the radical individualism of preachers who want to preach only their favorite biblical texts. The *Book of Common Prayer* (BOC) obliges Anglicans to hear all of Scripture read in worship over a three-year cycle. Though we've always had mavericks, the liturgy discourages such.

In some sense, then, the BOC is Anglicanism's teaching office. Methodists use hymns in much the same way. Other traditions use preaching. For Anglicans, traditionally it's been the liturgy.

Perhaps the most distinctive feature of Anglicanism is its emphasis on the via media, the middle way. Is that still important?

Historically it's been very important. Though it is implicit in Cranmer, it doesn't become articulated as such until Richard Hooker (c. 1544–1600), in his *Treatise on the Laws of Ecclesiastical Polity.* He argues that Anglicanism follows a middle way, retaining the best of Roman Catholicism (liturgy and tradition) and Protestantism (authority of Scripture and justification by faith).

Recently, in a book called *The Renewal of Anglicanism*, I argue that a more helpful middle way today would run between fundamentalism and liberalism. Anglicanism at its best avoids fundamentalism, which rejects culture, and liberalism, which accommodates itself too much to culture.

For both Episcopalians in the United States and Anglicans in Britain, the real opponents are no longer other Protestants or Roman Catholics but unbelievers, and these unbelievers are looking for a Christian faith that is distinctive but not culture rejecting.

What is the state of Anglicanism in England today? Some reports suggest that only 2 percent of Anglicans attend church.

It varies from one region to another, and certainly, the horror story of the 2 percent would apply in some inner-city areas. But in general, church attendance is much higher than that, perhaps averaging between 15 and 20 percent. The Church of England, because it is a state church, has always had this gap between official membership and the committed.

There is much evidence that Anglicanism is being renewed by various evangelical and charismatic groups. On the other hand, we seem to have a reluctance to recognize that certain beliefs and practices are simply non-Christian or anti-Christian. Some bishops have argued publicly for the ordination of homosexuals or against the bodily resurrection of Jesus. When a bishop is consecrated, the bishop is asked to defend the orthodox faith. Though we have the ability to enforce more theological conformity, we don't seem to be doing that.

What about internationally? Today there are more Anglicans worshipping in Africa than in America, Canada, and Australia combined.

The big growth area for Anglicanism is in Africa and Asia, where Anglicanism has not been tainted by the Enlightenment and Western culture. In Africa, Anglicanism is dynamic and vibrant, not cerebral and reserved. It's not a Western form of Anglicanism at all. The Western form of Anglicanism has accommodated itself to Western culture. Maybe the time has come for Africans to send missionaries to North America and to Europe.

Is it time to update the liturgy again? Is there a need for a new Thomas Cranmer, a new Book of Common Prayer?

In 1980, we updated our liturgy by adding a supplementary book called *Alternative Service Book*, which includes updated liturgics. So there has been a move toward liturgical renewal.

But that's been going on for over fifteen years now, and in many quarters there's a certain weariness with liturgical innovation. Many people find innovation quite unsettling. They do like some guidelines, some norms regarding public worship. But who knows what the future holds?

In your study of Cranmer and the English Reformation, what are you especially thankful for?

Cranmer has helped me put into words what I feel about Communion. In his *Book of Common Prayer*, he used some very powerful phrases to describe the meaning of the death of Christ and its importance to us. His phrases tend to stick in the mind and act as triggers to theological reflection.

Let me give you one small example. In the service, we thank God that in Communion he is "assuring us of thy gracious favor." To me, that is a very helpful phrase, and it triggers a Lutheran turn of thought in me. It reminds me that one of the functions of the sacrament is to reassure me of the total trustworthiness of God and his love for us in Christ.

There are many such phrases throughout the liturgy that act in this way on me. I'm thankful for Cranmer's ability to express the wonders of the gospel in such memorable words.

John Calvin Further Defines the Principles of Protestantism

by Alister McGrath

John Calvin was the second key leader in the Protestant Reformation, after Martin Luther. His *Institutes of the Christian Religion*, published in 1536, was the most inclusive and systematic presentation of the Christian faith as held by Protestants. The book covered four major aspects of this faith, dealing with God the Father, Jesus Christ, the Holy Spirit, and the church. It was in the third area that Calvin discussed predestination, the idea that even before creation God chose some people to be saved. Even though many other reformers held to an identical belief, Calvin's careful explanation of this idea permanently linked his name with the concept. His book also emphasized God's sovereignty, thus arguing that no person can demand our ultimate loyalty. As a result, he is seen by many to be the father of democracy.

In the excerpt that follows, Alister McGrath, a professor at Oxford and author and editor of many magazines and books, focuses on why Calvin should be considered one of the most influential people of the thousand years between A.D. 1000 and 2000. McGrath explores Calvin's belief in a strong work ethic and an active engagement in the affairs of the world, which broke with the medieval concept of separation from the world. Calvin's beliefs led to modern Christianity's forceful, positive influences on political and social matters.

The sixteenth century was a period of tumultuous change in Western Europe. The need for some kind of moral and intellectual shake-up within the church had been obvious for some time. Many religious and political writers of the fifteenth century had been aware of the weaknesses of the medieval church and the society in which it was embedded. However, there are good reasons for thinking that few were really prepared for the radical events of the sixteenth century, which are generally referred to collectively as "the Reformation.". . .

In taking a retrospective look at the second millennium, it is . . . both inevitable and entirely proper to explore the continuing impact of the Reformation, particularly concerning religion and public life. Three figures would immediately suggest themselves as candidates for discussion. Martin Luther (1483–1546) and Huldrych Zwingli (1484–1531) represent the first phase of the Reformation, John Calvin (1509–64) the second.

Calvin's task can be thought of as consolidation rather than initiation. The first phase of the Reformation focused on issues relating to personal salvation and the need for reform in the life of the church. Although Calvin never lost sight of these themes, he is perhaps best remembered for his detailed exposition of the leading themes of the Reformed faith in his *Institutes of the Christian Religion*—widely regarded as the most significant religious work of the sixteenth century—and his wrestling with issues concerning the identity of the church and its place in public life. This second aspect of his thinking developed against the all-important background of the life of the city of Geneva [Switzerland], which can be thought of as the laboratory within which Calvin forged his new ideas.

Calvin has excited a variety of responses, both from those who read him and from those who only read about him. He has been the object of much attention from theologians, church leaders, and historians. Some of that attention has been uncritical and laudatory; in that view, Calvin is the man who got (virtually) nothing wrong. For others, Calvin was the "dictator of Geneva," a personally unattractive person who got (virtually) nothing right. Neither approach is of much value in understanding the man and his legacy. . . .

Calvin understood Christianity as a faith that engages the realities of both personal and public life. He had considerable interest in the development of an authentic Christian theology, and was well aware of the importance of issues of personal piety and spirituality. Yet his vision of the Christian faith extended far beyond the piety of a privatized faith or the cerebral conundrums of an intellectualized theology. Theology for Calvin offered a framework for engaging with public life.

Calvin and Economic Ideas

A culture of free enterprise flourished in Geneva, in large part thanks to Calvin's benign attitude towards economics and finance. . . .

Calvin . . . was perfectly aware of the financial realities at Geneva and their implications. Although he did not develop an "economic theory" in any comprehensive sense of the term, he appears to have been fully cognizant of basic economic principles, recognizing the productive nature of both capital and human work. He praised the division of labor for its economic benefits and the way it emphasizes human interdependence and social existence. The right of individuals to possess property, denied by the radical wing of the Reformation, Calvin upheld. He recognized that passages in the Book of Deuteronomy relating to business ethics belonged to a bygone age; he refused to let the rules of a primitive Jewish agrarian society have binding force upon the progressive, modern, and urban Geneva of his time. Calvin dealt with the absolute prohibition upon lending money at interest (usury), for example, by arguing that it was merely an accommodation to the specific needs of a primitive society. Since there was no similarity between such a society and Geneva—interest is merely rent paid on capital, after all—he allowed lenders to charge a variable rate of interest. Calvin was sensitive to the pressures upon capital in a more or less free market, and believed that the ethical aims of the usury prohibition could be safeguarded by other means.

The Work Ethic

Calvin also articulated a work ethic that strongly encouraged the development of Geneva's enterprise culture. He taught that the individual believer has a vocation, to serve God in the world—in every sphere of human existence—lending a new dignity and meaning to ordinary work. Calvin agreed that the world should be treated with contempt to the extent that it is not God, and is too easily mistaken for him; yet, it is the creation of God, to be affirmed at least to a degree. "Let believers get used to a contempt of the present life that gives rise to no hatred of it, or ingratitude towards God. . . . Something that is neither blessed nor desirable in itself can become something good for the devout." Christians are thus to inhabit the world with joy and gratitude, without becoming trapped within it. A degree of critical detachment must accompany Christian affirmation of the world as God's creation and gift. Christians are to live in the world, while avoiding falling into that world, becoming immersed within and swallowed by it. . . .

Scholars are much divided about the spiritual status of work in the Middle Ages. The Benedictine model of monasticism, with its stress on *ora et labora* [pray and work], undoubtedly attributed great dignity to manual labor, though the first duty of the monk was always the Divine Office, called his "Opus Dei" [work of God]. It has been urged by some that the Benedictines, with their vast network of monastic enterprises, were in fact "the first capitalists." However that may be, there also persisted a widespread perception in medieval Christianity that those who worked "in the world," as distinct from monastics and clerics more generally, were engaged in a less worthy way of life and, indeed, were second-class Christians. Certainly that perception, combined with various corruptions of monasticism so caustically criticized by Erasmus and others, led Reformers such as Luther and Calvin to sharply contrast the monastic call "from the world" with the authentically Christian call "into the world."

In this view, Christians were called to be priests to the world, purifying and sanctifying its everyday life from within. Luther stated this point succinctly when commenting on Genesis 13:13: "What seem to be secular works are actually the praise of God and represent an obedience which is well-pleasing to him." There were no limits to this notion of calling. Luther even extolled the religious value of housework, declaring that although "it has no obvious appearance of holiness, yet these very household chores are more to be valued than all the works of monks and nuns."

A Vocation or "Calling"

Underlying this new attitude is the notion of the vocation or "calling." God calls his people, not just to faith, but to express that faith in quite definite areas of life. Whereas monastic spirituality regarded vocation as a calling out of the world into the desert or the monastery, Luther and Calvin regarded vocation as a calling into the everyday world. The idea of a calling or vocation is first and foremost about being called by God, to serve him within his world. Work was thus seen as an activity by which Christians could deepen their faith, leading it on to new qualities of commitment to God. Activity within the world, motivated, informed, and sanctioned by Christian faith, was the supreme means by which the believer could demonstrate his or her commitment and thankfulness to God. To do anything for God, and to do it well, was the fundamental hallmark of authentic Christian faith. Diligence and dedication in one's everyday life are, Calvin thought, a proper response to God.

For Calvin, God places individuals where he wants them to be, which explains Calvin's criticism of human ambition as an unwillingness to accept the sphere of action God has allocated to us. Social status is an irrelevance, a human invention of no spiritual importance;

one cannot allow the human evaluation of an occupation's importance to be placed above the judgment of God who put you there. All human work is capable of "appearing truly respectable and being considered highly important in the sight of God." No occupation, no calling, is too mean or lowly to be graced by the presence of God.

The work of believers is thus seen to possess a significance that goes far beyond the visible results of that work. It is the person working, as much as the resulting work, that is significant to God. There is no distinction between spiritual and temporal, sacred and secular work. All human work, however lowly, is capable of glorifying God. Work is, quite simply, an act of praise—a potentially productive act of praise. Work glorifies God, it serves the common good, and it is something through which human creativity can express itself. The last two, it must be stressed, are embraced by the first. As Calvin's English follower William Perkins put it, "The true end of our lives is to do service to God in serving of man."

This insight is important in assessing certain aspects of the Reformation work ethic. Calvin, for example, weighs in strongly in support of St. Paul's injunction, "If someone does not work, then he should not eat" (2 Thessalonians 3:10). Several modern writers have severely criticized Calvin for that view, arguing that his comments demonstrate his insensitivity to the needs of the unemployed. Calvin's primary target, however, appears to have been quite different: the French aristocrats who sought refuge in Geneva and felt that their social status placed them above the need to work. They would not work; for Calvin, the common human obligation is to labor in the garden of the Lord, in whatever manner is commensurate with one's God-given gifts and abilities on the one hand, and the needs of the situation on the other. The common obligation to work is the great social leveler, a reminder that all human beings are created equal by God.

In many ways, Calvin's work ethic can be seen as a development of Paul's injunction to the Corinthian Christians: "Each one should retain the place in life that the Lord assigned to him and to which God has called him" (1 Corinthians 7:17). Calvin emphasized that the everyday activity of ordinary Christians has deep religious significance. The English poet George Herbert expressed this insight eloquently:

> Teach me, my God and King,
> In all things thee to see;
> And what I do in anything
> To do it as for thee.
> A servant with this clause
> Makes drudgery divine;
> Who sweeps a room, as for thy laws,
> Makes that and the action fine.

The Value of Calvin Today

So who can learn from Calvin today? It is ironic that those who perhaps are most willing to listen to Calvin are also those who have most to learn from him. American evangelicalism is a complex phenomenon, and I have no wish to misrepresent it through simplification. However, it is fair to say that most evangelicals—and I write as one who gladly and positively identifies with this movement—regard the sixteenth-century Reformation as a period of heroic renewal of the Christian faith and triumphant rediscovery of the meaning of Scripture.

Yet many American evangelicals are ambivalent about engaging—as Calvin urged—with social and political matters. To become involved in such affairs is, they fear, to compromise the integrity of one's faith, to risk contamination by the sin of the world. Faith is a private matter, and is best kept that way. In making these observations, I must stress that I am not dismissing them; they represent serious concerns that reflect a perceptive appreciation of what can all too easily happen through uncritical immersion in the affairs of the world.

Calvin encourages believers to get involved—to be salt in the world. For Calvin, it is entirely possible to maintain integrity of faith while injecting a Christian presence and influence within society. This vision of a Christian society held a powerful appeal to our forebears: John Winthrop (1588–1649), the first Puritan governor of Massachusetts, even sought to build on the basis of the gospel a Christian civilization in the New World. Perhaps that vision lies beyond our reach—but it remains a challenge and stimulus to our thinking. . . .

Calvin reminds his modern-day successors that while such engagement runs many risks, it is essential nonetheless if Christians are to be the leaven where leavening is most needed. It is not merely evangelicals who need to hear this counsel. If Christianity is to remain a positive force and influence in American public life, all Christians need to be present within that life, as salt and light. To remain safely behind the barricades may seem more secure, and a lot less risky—but it denies us any chance of reforming, renewing, and recalling our culture. The legacy of John Calvin invites us to engage our world, and instructs us in how to do so with integrity.

The Great Awakening Gives Christianity a Uniquely American Identity

by Winthrop S. Hudson

Religious and political life in the American colonies was strongly influenced in the 1700s by the so-called Great Awakening, part of a larger evangelical Christian movement that swept the English-speaking world into the late 1800s. The movement involved a new style of preaching and public worship, and the rise of the revival meeting to reach people. Membership in the church depended less on adherence to broad religious doctrines and more on evidence of individual religious experience, a trend that continues today: Conservative American Protestantism still has the revivalist character that emerged during the 1700s. Many historians believe that the Great Awakening unified the colonies and encouraged them to throw off political as well as religious tradition, leading them to declare independence from England.

Winthrop S. Hudson, professor of church history at the University of Chicago, explains in the following excerpt the role of George Whitefield in creating a unified movement in America. Hudson follows the religious changes in the colonies during this period and discusses the religious and political consequences of the Awakening.

John Corrigan and Winthrop S. Hudson, *Religion in America*, 7th Edition. Upper Saddle River, NJ: Pearson, 2004. Copyright © 2004 by the publisher. Reproduced by permission.

It was not until 1740 that the local manifestations of intense religious interest and concern were transformed into a Great Awakening which was to spread throughout every colony from Nova Scotia to Georgia and to touch every area—urban and rural, tidewater and backcountry—and every class—rich and poor, educated and uneducated—before its power was finally dissipated. There had been interconnections, to be sure, between [earlier] revival movements. . . . But these were mostly tenuous connections and the revivals remained local in character until they were consolidated into a single movement by the itinerant activity of George Whitefield.

"The Grand Itinerant"

A recent graduate of Oxford University, where he had been an intimate friend of the Wesleys [Charles, creator of famous hymns, and John, founder of Methodism] and a member of the "Holy Club," Whitefield had spent a few months in Georgia in 1738. Upon his return to England he had adopted, much to the dismay of John Wesley, the expedient of preaching in the open air. Since both men had come to look upon "all the world" as their "parish" to the extent that they were convinced that wherever they chanced to be it was their "bounden duty to declare unto all that are willing to hear the glad tidings of salvation," Whitefield's expedient had the distinct advantage of making it unnecessary to secure an invitation from a local church in order to have an opportunity to preach. Moreover Whitefield's preaching in the open air met with such success that by the time he returned to America late in 1739 he had persuaded Wesley to "become more vile" and to preach in his stead to the great throngs he had assembled in the vicinity of Bristol.

Whitefield arrived in Philadelphia on November 2, 1739. He was a "slim slender youth," twenty-four years of age, with a strong but mellow voice, perfect enunciation, a keen sense of the dramatic, and an ability by subtle inflection to clothe almost any word with emotion. Later it was said that by merely pronouncing the word "Mesopotamia" he could bring tears to the eyes of his listeners. Although his intention had been to proceed immediately to Georgia to look after the affairs of his projected orphanage, Whitefield was prevailed upon to preach first in the Anglican church, then in other churches, and finally he spoke to great crowds each evening from the steps of the courthouse. The response was astonishing. Even Benjamin Franklin was impressed, both with the young man himself and with the good moral effect of his preaching. William Tennent [American Presbyterian minister and educator] visited him and persuaded him to make a rapid evangelistic tour of the area between Philadelphia and New York, which had already been stirred by revivals. Conscious of the new opportunity that had opened before him, Whitefield determined to preach his way to Georgia, traveling by land instead of going by ship. After a brief period in Savannah, he was back in the Philadelphia area from the middle of April to the middle of May to collect funds for the building of his orphanage, announcing his intention to visit New England in the autumn on a similar mission.

Whitefield arrived at Newport, Rhode Island, on September 14, 1740, having sailed from Charleston three weeks before. His arrival had been well publicized, and the Boston newspapers carried advertisements of numerous books and tracts by and about Whitefield and even called attention to other writings which he approved. During the next seventy-three days he was to travel eight hundred miles and to preach one hundred and thirty sermons. He was met everywhere by great throngs. The ministers of Boston were enthusiastic in the welcome they extended (Charles Chauncy [American Congregational clergyman] may have had some reservations), Harvard and Yale threw open their doors, the visit to Jonathan Edwards [American philosophical theologian and president of Princeton] at Northampton was a triumphant pilgrimage, and by the time Whitefield had made his way through New York and New Jersey to Philadelphia he was convinced that America was to be his "chief scene of action." While this was not to be true, he did make three other tours of the colonies and had just embarked upon a fourth when he died at Newburyport, Massachusetts, on September 30, 1770.

If America was not the chief scene of his labors, Whitefield nonetheless did as much to shape the future of American religious life as anyone else. Previous to his coming the "quickening" sermons had been preached in churches and at stated hours of public worship. And when sermons were delivered to congregations other than one's own it was at the invitation of the pastor. But Whitefield knew no such restrictions. He preached whenever and wherever he could find anyone to listen; and in this, as well as in his extemporaneous preaching, he had many imitators. Through him also, with his incessant traveling and a catholicity of spirit that welcomed an opportunity to preach from any pulpit that was opened to him, the revival impulse permeated every denomination. . . .

In the South the Awakening developed more slowly. Although Whitefield preached to large numbers in the South, the way had not been prepared for him by earlier revivals and there was little leadership to conserve the results he obtained. The old established areas of Virginia were Anglican territory and the Anglican clergy were unsympathetic and even hostile. The other areas were more recently settled and, without a modicum of leisure and existing centers of church life, there had been scant opportunity for revivals to develop. Thus throughout the South it was Whitefield who blazed the way for the spread of the Awakening instead of consolidating existing interest into a single movement as he had done elsewhere.

The earliest indication of a spiritual quickening in Virginia occurred east of the mountains in Hanover county. As a result of Whitefield's influence as he made his way overland to Georgia in December, 1739, a few lay people had begun to meet in private homes to read some of Whitefield's sermons and other devotional literature. A spontaneous revival broke out. As religious concern spread, the homes of the leaders became too small to hold the gatherings and "reading houses" were erected. This was the situation when William Robinson (d. 1746), a graduate of William Tennent's "log college," was sent by the New Brunswick Presbytery on a missionary tour of Virginia during the winter of 1742–43. Those who had erected the "reading houses" invited him to preach and were persuaded by him to become Presbyterians. Robinson was followed by a succession of revivalist itinerants sent out by the Synod of New York and its subsidiary presbyteries, the most important of whom was to be Samuel Davies who succeeded Robinson at Hanover in 1747. Under his leadership the revival spread rapidly, numerous churches were organized, which were brought together in 1755 to form a new presbytery. After Davies' departure in 1759 to become president of Princeton, the Presbyterian activity became less pronounced.

In the meantime the revival had broken out in another quarter. Two brothers-in-law, Shubal Stearns and Daniel Marshall (1706–84), had come to Virginia from New England in 1754. They had been converted by Whitefield, had become Separate Congregationalist itinerants, and then had been ordained as Baptist preachers. Within a year of their arrival in Virginia they were told of a large tract across the border in North Carolina where there was no preaching of any kind and the people "so eager to hear that they would come forty miles each way when they could have opportunity to hear a sermon." Here at Sandy Creek a church was gathered. In three years two additional churches had been formed, and in seventeen years there were forty-two churches. Daniel Marshall went on to Georgia where he labored with almost equal success, and throughout the whole Piedmont region, but especially in Virginia, Separate Baptist churches multiplied at an astonishing rate. . . .

As Hanover was the center of Presbyterian expansion, and Sandy Creek the center from which radiated Baptist evangelistic activity, so Dinwiddie County was to be the center of the revival impulse among the Anglicans. It was a delayed response, for no leader appeared until Devereux Jarratt (1733–1801) was installed in 1763 as rector at Bath. He had been influenced in his early years by Whitefield, and when he went to England for ordination he had come into contact with both Whitefield and John Wesley. Under Jarratt's zealous preaching his three churches became so crowded that he was compelled to hold services in adjacent groves, and he followed the precedent of Whitefield and Wesley in meeting with the more earnest Christians in small groups.

As early as 1765 two of John Wesley's lay preachers had come to America as immigrants—Robert Strawbridge (d. 1781) to Maryland and Philip Embury (1728–73) to New York. They were followed by two others who arrived in 1769, and in the same year Wesley commissioned the first two of eight officially appointed lay missionaries to serve in America. In 1772 Robert Williams, one of Wesley's lay preachers, appeared in Dinwiddie County and enlisted Jarratt's participation in a more widespread endeavor. Jarratt began to itinerate beyond the bounds of his own parish and the great assemblies gathered in the open air to hear him preach were impressive. Jesse Lee, one of his young converts, reported:

> I have been at meetings where the whole congregation would be bathed in tears, and sometimes their cries would be so loud that the preacher's voice could not be heard. Some would be seized with trembling and in a few moments drop on the floor as if they were dead, while others were embracing each other with streaming eyes and all were lost in wonder, love, and praise.

With the assistance of several lay preachers, Jarratt was busily forming converts into "methodist" societies, and as a result of his activity the great strength of the revival movement among the Anglicans was to be found in Virginia and the adjoining counties of North Carolina. By 1777 there were 4,379 members of the societies in this area, while the total for all the colonies was only 6,968. . . .

The Awakening was much more than the activity of a few conspicuous leaders. It was "Great" because it was general. People everywhere were caught up in the movement, and its influence was spread by innumerable local pastors, passing itinerants, and lay exhorters. No one could escape the excitement or avoid the necessity to declare himself as friend or foe.

And because the Awakening was general, it played an important role in forming a national consciousness among people of different colonies whose primary ties were with Europe rather than with one another. As a spontaneous movement which swept across all colonial boundaries, generated a common interest and a common loyalty, bound people together in a common cause, and reinforced the conviction that God had a special destiny in store for America, the Awakening contributed greatly to the development of a sense of cohesiveness among the American people. It was more influential in this respect than all the colonial wars the colonists were called upon to fight, more influential in fact than many of the political squabbles they had had with the mother country since the latter as often served to separate as to unite them. Whitefield, Tennent, and Edwards were rallying names for Americans a full three decades before Washington, Jefferson, Franklin, and Samuel Adams became familiar household names. Perhaps it is significant that the Awakening did not reach Nova Scotia until 1776, too late to create the intangible ties which bound the other colonies together.

Institutional Consequences

No exact estimate can be made of members added to the churches by the Awakening, but the number in all denominations was large. Interest in Indian missions was revived. A wide variety of charitable projects, including schools for Indians, Negroes, and the children of indentured servants, were initiated. The role of the laity in the churches was enhanced. . . .

Apart from the multiplication of churches, the major institutional survivals of the Awakening came from the impulse that was given to higher education by the necessity to provide educational opportunities for the swelling number of ministerial recruits. The Presbyterians were especially active in this endeavor and many of their ministers established classical academies, similar in character to William Tennent's "Log College" and patterned after the small private Presbyterian academies of Ireland and the Dissenting academies of England which at this time enjoyed an educational reputation that was greater than that of the ancient universities. Several colleges—Washington and Lee, Washington and Jefferson, and Dickinson—trace their ancestry back to these early academies. In 1746 the Synod of New York secured a charter for the College of New Jersey (Princeton) which was designed as the capstone of the Presbyterian educational structure, and in 1776 the Hanover Presbytery in Virginia established Hampden-Sydney College. The Baptists also organized several academies and in 1764 founded the College of Rhode Island (Brown University) as their major center for the training of the ministry. In 1766 the prorevivalists among the Dutch Reformed obtained a charter for Queen's College (Rutgers University). Dartmouth, an outgrowth of an Indian charity school, was incorporated in 1769. . . .

Although the clergy of the English settlements along the seaboard did not have the opportunity to duplicate the work of the priests who accompanied the French traders and trappers on their far-ranging travels through the interior of the continent, the evangelization of those tribes with whom the English came into contact did not suffer neglect. The effect of the Awakening was to pour new enthusiasm into this task. Eleazar Wheelock, Samuel Kirkland, David Brainerd, and for a time Jonathan Edwards were among those who devoted themselves to Indian missions. The diary of David Brainerd, edited by Jonathan Edwards, is a moving testament of devotion which tells the story of his experiences among the Indians, and it inspired many others to give themselves to mission work. . . .

Unity

Although the Awakening was productive of controversy and strife, it was, paradoxically, at the same time a great unifying force which, [according to historian Leonard Trinterud,] gave to "four-fifths" of the Christians in America "a common understanding of the Christian life and the Christian faith." Since the revival had penetrated many denominations quite indiscriminately, this common understanding tended to minimize the importance of denominational distinctions and to provide a basis for mutual respect, appreciation, and cooperation. Typical of the new spirit was John Wesley's emphatic declaration that he renounced and detested all distinctions among Christians, and refused to be distinguished from other men by anything but "the common principles of Christianity." From "real Christians" he had no desire to be distinguished at all. "Dost thou love and fear God? It is enough! I give thee the right hand of fellowship." This catholicity of spirit was even more conspicuously exhibited in George Whitefield. Whitefield spoke with equal readiness from Anglican, Presbyterian, Congregational, Baptist, and Dutch Reformed pulpits, and he counted men of all denominations among his converts. Preaching from the courthouse balcony in Philadelphia, he raised his eyes to the heavens and cried out:

> Father Abraham, whom have you in heaven? Any Episcopalians? No! Any Presbyterians? No! Any Independents or Methodists? No, no, no! Whom have you there? We don't know those names here. All who are here are Christians. . . . Oh, is this the case? Then God help us to forget party names and to become Christians in deed and truth. . . .

On the basis of this understanding of the Church which acknowledged the unity that existed within the diversity of outward ecclesiastical forms, the Protestant churches were able to develop a functional catholicity which was to find expression in the creation of a whole system of cooperative societies for the promotion of a host of worthy causes, including both home and foreign missionary activity. These were to be the instruments into which much of the evangelical fervor released by the Awakening was to be channeled when the Protestant churches subsequently addressed themselves to the overwhelming task of attempting to Christianize a whole continent.

William Carey Launches the Modern Christian Missionary Movement

by Brian Stanley

Christian churches had a long history of sporadic missionary endeavors among various peoples around the world. But it was not until William Carey's efforts in the 1790s that the modern missionary movement was launched. This movement, one of the most extensive religious movements in human history, transformed Christianity from a local, Western European church to a true world religion.

In this article, church historian Brian Stanley explains how Carey's ability to establish broad programs of Christian social, educational, and evangelistic activities in non-Christian lands won him the title "Father of Modern Missions." Brian Stanley is a lecturer in church history at Trinity College in Bristol, England, and the author of *The Bible and the Flag: Protestant Missions and British Imperialism in the Nineteenth and Twentieth Centuries.*

England in the 1790s was in the grip of a mixture of fear and excitement: fear, because just across the Channel in France a revolution had not only overthrown the monarchy, but seemed bent on destroying the Christian religion as well; mounting excitement, because Christians felt nonetheless that these upheavals might herald great events. Reports from France and later from Italy suggested that the days of the Roman Catholic Church —the Roman "Babylon" to English Protestants—might be numbered. Further afield, Captain James Cook's voyages had made Englishmen aware of exotic lands scarcely known before.

In England itself, Christians were praying. Starting in 1784, first Baptists and then other Nonconformists [Protestants who were not members of the Church of England] throughout the Midlands had been meeting for one hour on the first Monday of every month to pray for a revival which would lead to the spread of the gospel "to the most distant parts of the habitable globe." Confronted by political upheaval, widening geographical horizons and the new currents of spiritual life brought by the Evangelical Awakening, committed Christians began to suspect that God was about to do something radically new. Was the day prophesied in the Bible drawing near, the day of Christ's return? A young, Northamptonshire shoemaker named William Carey believed that it was, if only God's people persevered in their new commitment to prayer and began to translate that commitment into action.

William Carey

Carey had few obvious qualifications for the role he was about to fulfill. He was born in 1761 to a poor weaver in the village of Paulerspury. Largely self-educated, Carey became an apprentice shoemaker and, under the influence of a fellow apprentice, abandoned his Anglican family background to identify himself with the Nonconformists. He was baptized in 1783 and two years later became the pastor of a small Baptist church, supplementing his meagre stipend with school-teaching and work as a journeyman shoemaker.

From his boyhood Carey had been a voracious reader. At about the time of his baptism he read Captain Cook's *Voyages*—"the first thing that engaged my mind to think of missions," he later recalled. Above his work-bench hung a world map which he annotated with all the information he could discover regarding the different countries of the non-Christian world.

The spiritual state of those countries became his preoccupation. His friend Andrew Fuller records how Carey's heart "burned incessantly with desire for the salvation of the heathen." Few Christians of his day shared Carey's burning sense of responsibility for the millions who had never heard about Jesus Christ. At the fraternal meeting of the Northamptonshire Association of Baptist ministers in 1785, Carey raised for discussion the question, "Was not the command given to the Apostles, to teach all nations, obligatory on all succeeding ministers to the end of the world, seeing that the accompanying promise was of equal extent?" This was a novel interpretation of Jesus' command to preach the gospel to the world. Protestants had always insisted that the office of apostle had been given for the first century only, and that it was to the apostles that the Great Commission had been given. If God chose to convert the heathen, he would have to do so by conferring the same miraculous gifts which had accompanied the preaching of the gospel in the apostolic age and had died out with its passing. Carey's impertinent question therefore received a less than enthusiastic response.

Carey's Pamphlet

Faced with such complacency, Carey began in 1788 to plan a pamphlet setting out his conviction that the commission to "preach the gospel to every creature" was obligatory on all Christians for all time; it was therefore the "bounden duty" of the church in his day to attempt to bring the message of salvation in Christ to the whole world. Even Carey's closest ministerial associates—Andrew Fuller, John Sutcliff and John Ryland—still raised objections "on the ground of so much needing to be done at home, etc.," yet they urged him to get his pamphlet written. It eventually appeared on 12 May 1792 under the elaborate title *An Enquiry into the Obligations of Christians, to use Means for the Conversion of the Heathens: in which the religious state of the different nations of the world, the success of former undertakings, and the practicability of further undertakings, are considered.* The key words in the title were "Obligations" and "Means." If the command of Christ to preach the gospel to every creature was still binding, and if the biblical prophecies were true, which spoke of God's purpose being to extend the kingdom of his Son among men, then, argued Carey, all Christians ought "heartily to concur with God in promoting his glorious designs." In their praying together, Christians had begun to fulfil the first condition for the outpouring of God's Spirit. What was now required was for them to do something about obtaining what they were praying for. It was no good sitting back expecting some miracle of providence to transport them across the world and equip them with foreign tongues. No, those Christians who had caught the missionary vision should organize themselves into a society to send missionaries and support them in their evangelistic work.

The *Enquiry* may have convinced the intellect, but Carey needed to move Christian hearts as well as persuade Christian minds. His opportunity came on 30 May 1792 when he was to preach to the Northamptonshire Baptist Association at Nottingham. Carey chose as his text words from Isaiah: "Enlarge the place of thy tent, and let them stretch forth the curtains of thine habitations: spare not, lengthen thy cords, and strengthen thy stakes. . . ." Carey saw a parallel between the centuries-old plight of the exiled nation of Judah—apparently forgotten by God—and the unproductive and desolate church of his own day; in the biblical promise of a new and wider destiny for Judah lay the promise of countless new members of the Christian family to be drawn from all over the world. Once again, however, Carey insisted that God's promise was also his command. God was about to do great things by extending the kingdom of Jesus throughout the nations, and therefore Christians must attempt great things in taking the gospel to the worlds: "Expect great things from God. Attempt great things for God." John Ryland found Carey's exposition so forcible that he would not have been surprised "if all the people had lifted up their voice and wept." Yet when it came to the business meeting the following morning nobody was willing to make a proposition. Carey seized Andrew Fuller by the hand in desperation, inquiring whether "they were again going away without doing anything?" That was all that was required. Before the meeting dispersed the following resolution had been

recorded in the minutes: "Resolved, that a plan be prepared against the next Ministers' meeting at Kettering,
for forming a Baptist Society for propagating the
Gospel among the Heathen." The "Particular Baptist
Society for the Propagation of the Gospel amongst the
Heathen"—or, the Baptist Missionary Society, as it became known—was duly formed at Kettering on 2 October 1792. John Thomas, a physician who had already served in India, volunteered to serve as the first
missionary to India. Carey announced he would and
his family would also serve there.

Carey in India

William Carey landed in India at Calcutta with his wife
and four children on 7 November 1793. If he had any
illusions about the magnitude of his task, they were
quickly dispelled. Though agreeably surprised by the
readiness of the Hindus to listen to Christian preaching, Carey soon realized that [the strict Hindu class hierarchy known as the] caste system—"perhaps . . . one
of the strongest chains with which the devil ever
bound the children of men"—would prove a formida-
ble obstacle to a Hindu being converted. Discourage-
ments accumulated rapidly. Money was short. By January 1794 Carey's wife was already exhibiting signs of
the mental illness which was to last for the rest of her
life, and in September of that year they lost their third
son with dysentery. Carey's missionary colleague, John
Thomas, took to living in grand style and fell into debt.
In 1795 Carey had his first taste of criticism from domestic supporters.

Faced with an almost total absence of financial sup-
plies from England, Carey had accepted a post as man-

ager of an indigo factory. This provided him and his family with a regular means of support, and also money to spare to devote to missionary purposes. Some English Baptists, however, were quick to criticize Carey for "engaging in affairs of trade," and even his associates on the home committee dispatched a letter "full of serious and affectionate caution." The pages of Carey's journal reflect his mounting sense of discouragement. "When I first left England," he wrote in April 1794, "my hope of the conversion of the heathen was very strong; but among so many obstacles it would utterly die away, unless upheld by God, having nothing to cherish it." Carey came to rely increasingly on the promises of the Bible: "Yet this is our encouragement, the power of God is sufficient to accomplish everything which he has promised, and his promises are exceedingly great and precious respecting the conversion of the heathens."

Carey had to wait seven years to see the promise of God come to fruition in his first converts. On 22 December 1800 at Serampore, the Danish settlement which had been the home of the mission since the previous January, four Hindus came to faith in Christ. One of them, Krishna Pal, was baptized the following Sunday; the others followed later. William Ward, who, together with Carey and Joshua Marshman, now made up the famous "Serampore Trio," wrote jubilantly in his journal: "Brother C. has waited till hope of his own success has almost expired: and after all, God has done it with perfect ease! Thus the door of faith is opened to the gentiles; Who shall shut it?"

At first, few followed the example of Krishna Pal and the others, but by 1821 the missionaries had baptized a total of 1,407 converts, about half of whom were Indian nationals. Ahead of his time, William Carey never returned to his native land.

By the time of his death in 1834, the missionary movement from Britain had acquired a dynamic far greater than the impetus deriving from its original power. Yet it would be wrong to cast Carey in the role of a pioneer overtaken by the movement he initiated. Rather, he was a forerunner whose missionary vision displayed a breadth and boldness which frequently embarrassed his contemporaries and immediate successors. At the heart of that vision was the conviction that the proclamation of the gospel of Jesus Christ was the chief duty of the church and the only hope of salvation for the world. . . .

Carey and his colleagues were pioneering a tradition of missionary involvement in education which has been of major significance throughout the Third World. In almost every case, such involvement originated in the same evangelistic ambition as motivated Carey. These hopes have rarely been fulfilled; they were not fulfilled in India, and it was not long before voices both in India and in England were dismissing educational work as futile.

In the long term, missionary education in India and Africa has had a consequence which Carey could never have foreseen: the recipients of mission education have been the pioneers of Indian and African independence. The most enduring educational achievement of the Serampore Trio was the foundation in 1818 of Serampore College. Marshman was the driving force behind the project, but all three members of the Trio shared the vision which was set out in the college prospectus. "If the gospel stands in India, it must be by native being opposed to native in demonstrating its excellence above all other systems." The primary goal of the college was to train Indians to be missionaries to their own people. However, the educational opportunities of the college were open to all, whether Christian or not. Carey was impressed by how many of the leaders of the Protestant Reformation had been scholars, whose Christian learning gradually transformed the thinking of Catholic Europe. Serampore College was intended to unleash "the Reformation of India." But the Trio's broad conception of a literary and scientific education founded on Christian principles found no echo in the minds of their superiors and supporters in England. English Baptists, who showed little enthusiasm for their own theological colleges, showed even less of an inclination to support a college in India which placed such emphasis on "unspiritual" knowledge. In terms of the exalted ideals of its founders, Serampore College was a failure.

Evangelizing Through Locals

But its failure must not be allowed to overshadow the significance of Carey's motivating belief that India could be evangelized effectively only by Indians. This view was apparent in embryo in the *Enquiry* pamphlet of 1792, and by 1817 was fully explicit: "India will never be turned from her idolatry to serve the true and living God," Carey wrote to John Ryland, "unless the grace of God rest abundantly on converted Indians to qualify them for mission work, and unless, by those who care for India, these be trained for and sent into the work. In my judgement it is on native evangelists that the weight of the great work must ultimately rest." After the baptism of Krishna Pal in 1800, the missionaries set out to encourage his gifts "to the uttermost so that he may preach the Gospel to his countrymen," and Pal duly became an evangelist first in Calcutta, and then in Assam. By the date of Carey's death in 1834, the Serampore Mission had founded nineteen mission stations, manned by fifty "missionaries," of whom only six had been sent out from Europe. Carey was deeply committed to giving responsibility to national Christians, thereby anticipating the principles of Henry Venn, Secretary of the Church Missionary Society from 1841 to 1872, who insisted that the goal of Western missions was to create national churches which were self-supporting, self-governing and self-extending. . . .

In his *Enquiry*, Carey had expressed the view that missionaries ought to take "every opportunity" of doing good to the people to whom they were sent. Once in India, Carey was as good as his word, ready to engage in such diverse activities as translations of Hindu literature, educational work, medical care, attempts to improve agricultural methods, and political agitation for the removal of inhumane practices such as sati (the custom of burning widows alive on their husbands' funeral pyres). Carey's "advanced" conception of missionary work probably contributed to the unhappy estrangement between the Serampore missionaries and the Baptist Missionary Society which marred his later years.

Carey himself regarded all aspects of his work as a direct response to the command of Christ "to endeavour by all possible methods to bring over a lost world to God." Nothing less was required if God's purpose was to be fulfilled—to destroy evil and establish the kingdom of Jesus among men. William Carey made many Christians of his day feel uncomfortable. His insistence on taking the Great Commission at its face value embarrassed pious men for whom obedience to the missionary call seemed ludicrous and impracticable. His independent spirit in India alarmed more timid souls in England whose understanding of missionary work bore little relation to reality. Yet he did more than any other man to awaken the conscience of Protestant Christians to the spiritual need of millions worldwide who had never heard of Jesus Christ. That was indeed a "great thing" for a humble Northamptonshire shoemaker to attempt. But Carey made the attempt out of his confidence in a God who can do great things. Many of the countries where the Christian church is at its strongest and most alive today are the areas which witnessed this missionary activity in the nineteenth century—proof indeed that Carey's confidence was not misplaced.

Pope John Paul II Champions Human Rights

by E.J. Dionne Jr.

Pope John Paul II died on April 2, 2005, ending his twenty-seven year papacy of the Roman Catholic Church. In the following selection E.J. Dionne Jr. evaluates John Paul II's accomplishments and legacy. He maintains that John Paul II's papacy was both liberal and conservative. In his policies outside the church, the pope was generally liberal, advocating religious tolerance, democracy, and human rights. Within the church, however, his policies were more conservative; for example, he rejected calls to allow women or noncelibate men to become priests. Despite these contradictions, Dionne insists that John Paul will ultimately be remembered as a champion of social justice and human dignity. E.J. Dionne Jr. is a columnist for the *Washington Post*, a senior fellow at the Brookings Institution, and a professor at Georgetown University. He covered the Vatican for the *New York Times* from 1984 to 1986.

Do you think of Pope John Paul II as the man who condemned "luxurious egoism" and "imperialistic monopoly"? Do you remember him as the friend of workers who asserted "the priority of labor over capital"? Do you honor him as the first Pope who visited a synagogue, who told Catholics to embrace Jews as "our elder brothers," and who condemned anti-Semitism "at any time and by anyone"? Do you regard him as the hero of human rights who helped bring down Communist dictatorships and battled the death penalty?

Or do you think of John Paul as the man who presided over the condemnation of theologians who questioned the Church's teachings (on birth control) or preached liberation theology? Do you see him as intransigent in refusing to allow questioning of the all-male celibate priesthood? Do you note the extent to which he has transformed the Church by appointing conservative bishops and by naming a College of Cardinals likely to keep Catholicism on a traditionalist path?

"A sign of contradiction" was a favorite John Paul phrase, and it might be said to define his papacy. In his effect on Roman Catholicism's relationship to the world, his achievement will be judged as liberal. But his impact on the Church he leads has to be seen as conservative. These terms are vexed, and John Paul himself would probably reject them—he'd insist on his own consistency in opposing both the Marxist and capitalist forms of materialism, in arguing that the spiritual is always primary, and in asserting that the Church's central obligation is to doctrinal clarity. But the Pope's version of consistency does not necessarily match that of the world that is judging him. That's the paradox at the heart of his papacy.

Grappling with Modernity

Take first John Paul's approach to the outside world. Before the Second Vatican Council [1962 to 1965] and the papacy of John XXIII [1958 to 1963], the Church decried modernity and liberalism, which many in the Church leadership condemned simply as "a sin." As Peter Steinfels has noted, Pope Pius IX [pope from 1846 to 1878] used the terms "pernicious," "perfidious," "perverse," and "a virus," to refer to liberal Catholicism. The pre-Vatican II Church, especially in the 1930s, was inclined toward support of authoritarian governments and worried that embracing religious liberty meant tolerating "error."

Vatican II changed that, marking a truce with the modern world and, for many Catholics, an opportunity to embrace it. The Church sided with religious tolerance, democracy, and human rights. It was a stance at once moral and practical. Moral for the obvious reasons. Practical because the Church was beginning to grow in parts of the world where it found itself in the minority, and being in the minority teaches the importance of minority rights.

Moreover, John XXIII believed profoundly in taking the world as he found it—which meant grappling creatively with modernity. "Distrustful souls," he wrote in December 1961, "see only darkness burdening the face of the earth. We prefer instead to reaffirm all our confidence in our Savior who has not abandoned the world which he redeemed. Indeed, we make our own the recommendation of Jesus that we learn to distinguish 'the signs of the times,' and we seem to see now in the midst of so much darkness more than a few indications that augur well for the fate of the church and of humanity." As Reverend Joseph A. Komonchak, the premier historian of the Council, noted in *Commonweal*, "The conviction that God was still present and active in the world, as in the church, lay behind his frequent remark that the church is not a museum of antiques but a living garden of life."

John Paul Embraced Tolerance

John Paul confirmed the historic shift that John initiated and Pope Paul VI [pope from 1963 to 1978] sustained. Precisely because John Paul is seen as a conservative, his acceptance of these changes almost certainly makes them irreversible. One can make a strong case that, 100 years from now, John Paul's most remembered achievements will be the "liberal" ones. He insisted upon the dignity of every human person and thereby campaigned for human rights, for social justice, and for the rights of workers and the poor. At Yad Vashem, he apologized for "the hatred, acts of persecution, and displays of anti-Semitism directed against the Jews by Christians." There was some debate over whether he said enough. For Jews and Catholics of a certain age, what he said was a breathtaking relief.

And his experiences reaffirmed, as the Second Vatican Council and John had understood, that religious tolerance had practical benefits for a Church taking root in the world's non-Christian regions. His visit to India in 1986 was a striking lesson in the importance of religious liberty to the future of the Church. Walls in Madras carried anti-Christian graffiti, including: go with christ. go get crucified. No wonder John Paul praised the "precious principle" of the Indian constitution, which "specifically includes the right 'to profess, practice, and propagate religion.'"

John Paul lived in dynamic tension with modernity. That is different from outright opposition. And he was obviously skilled at adapting a 2,000-year-old Church

to the realities of the times. He realized that a centralized papacy provided him with a platform no other religious leader could claim. The Pope may have no divi-
sions, as Joseph Stalin once sneered, but boy, could he
command media attention.

Proposing Debate on Politics and Economics

But his attitude toward modernity was not just about
method. One of his most important encyclicals was
Centesimus Annus, issued 100 years after Leo XIII's great
social encyclical, *Rerum Novarum*. *Centesimus* has to
rank as one of the most successful papal documents in
history. Rather than present a single line that Catholics
should pursue in the area of politics and economics, it
set the terms of debate among people of goodwill. John
Paul ruled out dictatorships and highly centralized
command economies. He also opposed capitalism
without social safety nets and safeguards. But he left
open a broad area for debate and experimentation. The
Pope's approach was principled but not ideological. He
was certainly egalitarian, but he did not demand absolute equality. He was open to the advantages of markets and to the positive uses of government. You could
be on the right, as long as you acknowledged the im-
perative of lifting up the poor. You could be on the left,
as long as you acknowledged the limits of the state and
the right of individuals to personal initiative.

The highest compliment to the document lay not in
the fact that so many were eager to say they agreed
with the Pope, but that partisans of so many different
viewpoints in the Church insisted that the Pope had
agreed with them. Ardent supporters of free markets,
such as Michael Novak, the conservative philosopher,

saw the document as vindication and a breakthrough for a Church that had often expressed a deep skepticism of capitalism. Supporters of social reform and social democracy emphasized the document's insistence on government's responsibility to relieve poverty and guarantee workers' rights. In some sense, both sides were right. As Father J. Bryan Hehir has said, the Pope's assessment "takes the market reality seriously and acknowledges values in it that John Paul's predecessors may have assumed but did not assert." Yet the Pope also saw the market's moral limits. As Hehir put it, the Pope argued that "many human needs are not met by the workings of the market," that "there are whole groups of people without the resources to enter the market," and that "there are goods that cannot and must not be bought and sold." In his most important document on the political economy, John Paul proposed not dogma but debate. He laid out guidelines and boundaries, not anathemas.

A Centralizing Papacy

If John Paul's story stopped here, his papacy would be about the triumph of liberal Catholicism. But that is not how we understand it, because, if so much of what the Pope did in relation to the world outside the Church was progressive, so much of what he did inside it was conservative. His was a centralizing papacy, a papacy that insisted upon a strict—his critics would say narrow—view of orthodoxy. John Paul closed off debate on the nature of the priesthood, refusing discussion of expanding its ranks to women and noncelibate men despite the great shortage of priests. In a Church that had relied on the work of nuns, many middle-class, educated women—especially in the United States—went into rebellion. He cracked down hard on dissent, dealing blows to what conservatives might call the North American heresy (about sex and birth control) and the South American heresy (about Marxism).

This did not go down well with theologians who insisted there was nothing heretical about their convictions. The Reverend Charles Curran, a well-liked, respected (and tenured) professor of moral theology at Catholic University, was condemned in the mid-'80s and told to leave the faculty for his critique of the Church's stance on—among other things—birth control. Liberal Catholic academics feared the threat to academic freedom. His home bishop backed him, too. "If Father Curran's status as a Roman Catholic theologian is brought into question," said Bishop Matthew Clark of Rochester, "I fear a serious setback to Catholic education and pastoral life in this country."

The Vatican condemned liberation theology, which emphasized Christians' obligation to shake up or overthrow unjust social structures. It was understandable that the Pope might see it as a kind of Christianized Marxism, given his profound mistrust of a system of thought that had left his native Poland in chains. Yet many progressive Latin American bishops at the time begged to differ. "Liberation theology is not a theology of violence or one that pushes toward violence," insisted Bishop Jose Ivo Lorscheiter of Santa Maria, Brazil. "It is not a theology that assumes or justifies Marxist ideology."

A New Fundamentalism

Dissention was not confined to the Americas. The condemnation of Swiss-born theologian Hans Kung struck a blow against a liberal thinker of worldwide reputation. In 1985, the Roman Catholic bishops of England and Wales issued a statement warning against "a lack of tolerance and a certain new fundamentalism" in the Church. The statement called for greater local autonomy and argued against what the bishops saw as a habit of referring to Rome "decisions which could be made locally."

But the local churches themselves have been profoundly changed by John Paul. The power to appoint is the power to control, and the Pope literally outlasted his adversaries. As liberals in the Church leadership passed on, John Paul replaced them with loyalists, minimizing dissent at the top. Emblematic of these changes were the Pope's appointments of John J. O'Connor as archbishop in New York City and Bernard F. Law as archbishop in Boston. (O'Connor has passed away, and Law left Boston for a Vatican post after he was widely criticized for his handling of the sex-abuse scandal.) The two were dubbed "Archbishops Law and Order" for their assigned roles of enforcing the Pope's version of orthodoxy on the restive American Church. There are now many more bishops like them.

The Pope's insistence on democracy outside the Church thus did not translate to democracy inside the Church. His skilled spokesman, Joaquin Navarro-Valls, once offered an aphorism to explain why. "Authority is a guarantee of unity," Navarro-Valls said. "Authority is also a guarantee of truth." It's also true that authority too readily invoked can spark dissent, and some of John Paul's "truths"—like the proposition that women may never, under any circumstances, become priests— were simply not accepted among liberal American Catholics.

Recovery of the Sacred

There is, of course, something profoundly dissatisfying about creating dueling balance sheets—the Liberal List and the Conservative List—in judging John Paul's papacy. There is a temptation to reduce all religion and spirituality to politics. But doing so ignores what John Paul saw as the heart of his mission: the recovery of the sacred in an often profane world. And, while the breathless commentaries after his death too readily resorted to Hollywood-style blather about John Paul, superstar, and the Pope's standing as a beatified rock idol, he did have something very close to that overworked word, charisma. The man cannot be reduced to his doctrine.

I was blessed—and I do mean to use that word—to cover the Pope as a journalist in the '80s. In my experience, at least, he was both powerful and serene. He could be warm and stern, mystical and down to earth, immensely worldly and thoroughly committed to the world beyond this one. Yeah, I liked the guy.

I was often asked if a Catholic covering the Pope could avoid bias. Naturally my answer is yes. But, putting aside a metaphysical discussion of what bias means in this context (or, for that matter, what I actually put into print), I concluded that my personal feelings were paradoxical: The more Catholic I felt, the tougher I was inclined to be on his papacy. About the Catholic Church I love, I have great anxieties about splits between left and right that deepened under John Paul. I worry about the declining number of priests and nuns and the dwindling ranks of clerics inspired by Vatican II. I worry about what my daughters will make of a Church that reserves so much power for men. I worry that the balance between free inquiry and doctrinal rigor has shifted too decisively in favor of a very particular definition of orthodoxy.

Yet I have little doubt about how John Paul's impact on his times will be judged. In the world's large struggles—over human rights and democracy, poverty and social justice, war and peace, life and death—the Pope, to use a quasi-Marxist phrase he would probably hate, put the Church on the right side of history.

CHAPTER 4

Christianity: Its Legacy and Its Future

How Has Christianity Influenced World History?

by Kenneth L. Woodward and Anne Underwood

The following article, by *Newsweek* religion writers Kenneth L. Woodward and Anne Underwood, names Jesus as the dominant figure in Western civilization and Christianity as the source or inspiration for most Western ideas, inventions, and values. It is thus hard to overstate the influence of Christianity on world history. Woodward and Underwood outline the most significant effects, beginning with the concept of life after death and including the role of monks in the transition from the medieval age to the modern age and the development of law and education. The authors point out that the influence of Christianity on historical events has often been mixed: Imperialism and colonialism and war in the name of the Christian God have caused as well as prevented suffering and destruction.

Historians did not record his birth. Nor, for 30 years, did anyone pay him much heed. A Jew from the Galilean hill country with a reputation for teaching and healing, he showed up at the age of 33 in Jerusalem during Passover. In three days, he was arrested, tried and

convicted of treason, then executed like the common-
est of criminals. His followers said that God raised him
from the dead. Except among those who believed in
him, the event passed without notice.

Two thousand years later, the centuries themselves
are measured from the birth of Jesus of Nazareth. At the
end of this year [1999], calendars in India and China,
like those in Europe, America and the Middle East, will
register the dawn of the third millennium. It is a con-
vention, of course: a fiction and function of Western
cultural hegemony that allows the birth of Jesus to
number the days for Christians and non-Christians
alike. For Christians, Jesus is the hinge on which the
door of history swings, the point at which eternity in-
tersects with time, the Savior who redeems time by
drawing all things to himself. As the second millennium draws to a close, nearly a third of the world's population claims to be his followers.

The Influence of Jesus on Western Culture

But by any secular standard, Jesus is also the dominant
figure of Western culture. Like the millennium itself,
much of what we now think of as Western ideas, inventions and values finds its source or inspiration in the religion that worships God in his name. Art and science,
the self and society, politics and economics, marriage
and the family, right and wrong, body and soul—all
have been touched and often radically transformed by
Christian influence. Seldom all at once, of course—and
not always for the better. The same Jesus who preached
peace was used to justify the Crusades and the Inquisition. The same gospel he proclaimed has underwritten
both democracy and the divine right of kings. Often

persecuted—even today—Christians have frequently persecuted others, including other Christians. As Pope John Paul II has repeatedly insisted, Christians cannot welcome the third millennium without repenting of their own sins.

This millennial moment invites historical reflection: how has Christianity shaped the way we think about God, about ourselves, about how individuals ought to live and the way that societies are to be organized? As scholars have long realized, there was little in the teachings of Jesus that cannot be found in the Hebrew Scriptures he expounded. From this angle, says theologian Krister Stendahl of Harvard Divinity School, "Christianity became a Judaism for the Gentiles." But the New Testament is primarily Scripture about Jesus— the Risen Christ as Lord. This message was something altogether new. Like a supernova, the initial impact of Christianity on the ancient Greco-Roman world produced shock waves that continued to register long after the Roman Empire disappeared.

A New Conception of God and the Afterlife

The first Christians were Jews who preached in the name of Jesus. But Jesus wasn't all that they preached. As Jewish monotheists, they believed in one God—the Father to whom Jesus was obedient unto death. But they also worshiped Jesus as his "only begotten Son" conceived through the power of the Holy Spirit. This experience of God as three-in-one was implicit in the New Testament, but defied efforts to fit into the traditional monotheistic mold. By "asking Greek questions of Hebrew stories," says theologian David Tracy of the University of Chicago Divinity School, the early church

fathers developed a doctrine of God that was—and remains—unique among world religions. "All monotheists tend to make God into a transcendent individual
standing outside time and outside all relationships,"
Tracy observes. "Now, as in modern physics, we are
coming to see that all of reality is interrelated. The doctrine of the Trinity says that even the divine reality in
all its incomprehensible mystery is intrinsically rela-
tional." In short, Christianity bequeathed to Western
culture a God who revealed himself definitively in the
person of Jesus, and who continues to redeem the
world by the work of the Holy Spirit. Time itself was
transformed: where the Greeks and Romans thought of
the universe as fixed and eternal, Christianity—building on the Hebrew prophets—injected into Western
consciousness the notion of the future as the work of
God himself.

To a world ruled by fate and the whims of capricious
gods, Christianity brought the promise of everlasting
life. At the core of the Christian faith was the assertion
that the crucified Jesus was resurrected by God and present in the church as "the body of Christ." The message
was clear: by submitting to death, Jesus had destroyed
its power, thereby making eternal life available to
everyone. This Christian affirmation radically changed
the relationship between the living and the dead as
Greeks and Romans understood it. For them, only the
gods were immortal—that's what made them gods.
Philosophers might achieve immortality of the soul, as
Plato taught, but the view from the street was that human consciousness survived in the dim and affectless
underworld of Hades. "The Resurrection is an enormous answer to the problem of death," says Notre
Dame theologian John Dunne. "The idea is that the

Christian goes with Christ through death to everlasting life. Death becomes an event, like birth, that is lived through."

Once death lost its power over life, life itself took on new meaning for believers. Sociologist Rodney Stark of the University of Washington sees dramatic evidence of this in the high Christian survival rates during the plagues that repeatedly hit the citizens of the ancient Roman Empire. "The Romans threw people out into the street at the first symptoms of disease, because they knew it was contagious and they were afraid of dying," says Stark. "But the Christians stayed and nursed the sick. You could only do that if you thought, 'So what if I die? I have life eternal.'"

Indeed, those who were martyred for the faith were revered as saints and heavenly "friends of God" who could intercede for the faithful below. Their bones became sacred relics, their tombs the sites of pilgrimage. Thus was the Christian cult of the saints born, a reverencing of the dead and their bodies that confounded Rome's elites. "You keep adding many corpses newly dead to the corpse [of Christ] of long ago," complained Emperor Julian, a fourth-century persecutor of Christians. "You have filled the whole world with tombs and sepulchers." Eventually, churches were built over the tombs of saints (the Vatican's Basilica of St. Peter is the most famous example) and cemeteries were turned into cities.

Inversion of Values

As the sign of the new religion, the cross signified much more than Christ's victory over death. It also symbolized an inversion of accepted norms. Suffering was noble rather than merely pathetic when accepted in imitation of the crucified Christ. Forgiveness—even of one's enemies—became the sign of the true Christian. More radically, Jesus taught that in the kingdom of God the last would be first, the first last. "In the New Testament, you find Jesus more among the beggars than the rulers, the sick than the healthy, the women and children than the conquerors, the prostitutes and lepers than the holy people," says Martin Marty, director of the Public Religion Project at the University of Chicago.

Christianity also challenged prevailing notions of the virtuous life. Where Aristotle had touted prudence, justice, courage and temperance as the virtues proper to the good life, Jesus emphasized the blessedness of humility, patience and peacemaking in his crowning Sermon on the Mount. Where the Buddha taught compassion as an attitude of the Enlightened, Jesus demanded deeds: "In truth I tell you, in so far as you did this to one of the least of these brothers of mine, you did it to me." In Roman times, Christian compassion was manifest in special concern for widows, orphans, the aged and infirm. When Saint Lawrence, an early Christian martyr and deacon of the nascent church, was ordered by Roman authorities to reveal the church's treasures, he showed them the hungry and the sick. Twenty centuries later, the same attitude can be seen in the work of exceptional contemporary figures (usually women) like Dorothy Day and Mother Teresa. "The idea," says Marty, is "the poor are my masters."

Discovering the Individual

If, as [Shakespearean scholar] Harold Bloom has lately argued, Shakespeare "invented the human" it can be said—with equal hyperbole—that Christianity "discovered" the individual. In the ancient world, individuals were recognized as members of tribes or nations or families, and conducted themselves accordingly. For Jews, this meant—as now—that one's relationship with God depends upon the prior covenant he has made with Israel as his chosen people. But the Gospels are replete with scenes in which Jesus works one on one, healing this woman's sickness, forgiving that man's sins and calling each to personal conversion. He invites Jews and Gentiles alike to enter God's kingdom. "Christianity discovers individuality in the sense that it stresses personal conversion," says Bernard McGinn, professor of historical theology at the University of Chicago Divinity School. "This is a crucial contribution to Western civilization because it releases the individual from the absolute constraints of family and society."

The sense of self deepened. Prayer became more personal. As Jesus himself taught, God could be addressed as "Abba"—the equivalent of "Dad." But as the possibility of intimacy with God increased, so did the interior sense of personal unworthiness. As a moralist, Jesus had set the bar high: those who even looked on another's wife with sexual desire, he declared, committed "adultery in the heart." With the evolution of the Roman Catholic Church came the practice of personal confession and repentance. And in the *Confessions* of Saint Augustine (354–430), we have the first great document in the history of what Stendahl has called "the introspective conscience of the West." A towering figure whose shadow stretched across the Middle Ages and touched a tormented Martin Luther, Augustine remains to this day the father of autobiography, the first great psychologist and the author who anticipated—by a millennium and a half—the modern novel's explorations of individual self-consciousness.

Redefining Male and Female

In Roman as in Jewish society, women were regarded as inherently inferior to men. Husbands could divorce their wives but wives could not divorce their husbands. In rabbinic circles, only males were allowed to study the Torah. Jesus challenged these arrangements. Although he called only men to be his apostles, Jesus readily accepted women into his circle of friends and disciples. He also banned divorce, except in cases of adultery.

The early Christians heeded his example. In its initial stages, at least, the church strove to become an egalitarian society: in Christ, wrote Paul, "there is neither Jew nor Greek, slave nor free man, male or female." Although Paul's household code for Christians (Ephesians 5:22–23) called for wives to be subordinate to their husbands, both were equally subject to God.

Christianity's appeal for women was a major reason that it grew so rapidly in competition with other religions of the Roman Empire. Then, as now, most Christians were women. The new religion offered women not only greater status and influence within the church but also more protection as wives and mothers. For one thing, the church did away with the common practice of marrying girls of 11 or 12 to much older men. The result was a stronger, "more symmetrical marriage," says sociologist Stark. For another, Christianity carried over from Jewish tradition a profound respect for marriage. Eventually, the Catholic Church made marriage a sacrament, declaring the bond between Christian husband and wife insoluble.

In an even more radical challenge to the social mores of the ancient world, the church made room for virgins—both male and female—who consecrated their lives to Christ. In this way, says McGinn, consecrated Christian virgins "broke the bonds by which families controlled the fate of their members"—especially women. Thus, Christianity made it possible for celibate females or males to claim a complete life and identity apart from marriage and procreation.

The church also protected children from the whims of tyrannical fathers. Under Roman law, fathers could and often did commit infanticide. Female babies were especially vulnerable because they were nothing but an expense. From a study of gravestones at Delphi, Stark says, we know that of 600 upper-class families, "only half a dozen raised more than one daughter." From the beginning, Christians also opposed abortion, defending both mother and child from barbarous procedures that often left women either dead or sterile.

In a less direct way, Christianity also transformed the way that masculinity was defined throughout the ancient world. In place of the dominant image of the male as warrior, Jesus counseled men to be peacemakers—to "turn the other cheek" rather than strike back. "A woman preaching that people must be patient and meek and mild would have sounded just like a woman," argues Michael Novak, who covers religion and public policy at the American Enterprise Institute—and, he implies, would have been dismissed by men. But to believe, as Christians did, that this was the Son of God speaking meant that Christians could never make war with a clear conscience.

Nonviolence was easy to espouse as long as Christians had no power. As Yale church historian Jaroslav

Pelikan observes, "They never imagined that Caesar might become a Christian"—which he did when Constantine converted in 312—much less that theirs would become the official religion of the Roman Empire. With establishment came the power to wage war and to stamp out heretics. From his imperial throne in Constantinople, Constantine did both as protector of the church. But in the West, as "eternal" Rome fell to invaders from the North, Augustine laid down severe restrictions if the conduct of war between states is to be considered just. Among other principles outlined in his monumental *The City of God*, Augustine said that only defensive wars could be justified. They should be brief, a last resort and never for spoils or gain. The means of war should never be excessive but always proportional to its goals. Noncombatants were to be immune from harm, and once the war was over, the aim of the winners was to be peace, not revenge.

While Augustine's just-war principles have never prevented wars from happening—including those waged in Jesus' name—they have, over the centuries, at least prompted some statesmen to try to make warfare less barbarous. We are still a long way from nonviolence. "But before Christ," notes Stark, "conquerors butchered people for the hell of it."

Ironically, once Christianity was identified with the state, many Christians found it more difficult to follow Christ than when they were a persecuted sect. To escape an increasingly worldly and compromised church, many Christian men and women fled to the desert (as some Jewish sects before them had done), where they could live in complete poverty, chastity and obedience. These became the basis of the Rule of Saint Benedict—"one of the most influential documents of Western civilization," according to Pelikan—which established monastic communities as places set apart for those called to fully "participate in the life of Christ."

The effects of monasticism on Western society can hardly be exaggerated. For more than a millennium, the monasteries produced saints who established the diverse forms of Christian mysticism and spirituality that are so much in revival today. The monks were also the church's reformers, calling popes to task for their worldliness and eventually becoming popes themselves. Through the example of the monks, celibacy became required of bishops in the East and, eventually, of all priests in the West.

Monks and Modernity

It was the monks who became Christianity's greatest missionaries, planting the church in England, Ireland and other outposts of no-longer eternal Rome. As the barbarians dismantled the empire, the monks copied and later disseminated the Latin classics, thus preserving much of the old civilization and laying the foundations of the new. They also created music and chants, magnificent liturgies and marvelous illuminated manuscripts. In the so-called Dark Ages—a fiction created by anti-religious philosophes of the French Enlightenment—it was the monks who founded the first European universities in cities like Paris and Bologna. It was a Dominican friar, Thomas Aquinas, who crowned the Middle Ages with his towering synthesis of philosophy and theology, the *Summa Theologica*. And it was another monk, Martin Luther, who fathered the Protestant Reformation.

One measure of Christian influence on Western culture is the extent to which innovations of the church have survived in secular form. The law is a prime example. "Much of medieval canon law has passed over—often unnoticed—into the laws of the state," says Harold Berman, professor of law emeritus at Harvard law school. "And many of the legal reforms the medieval papacy promoted command respect even seven and eight centuries later." Among them: rational trial procedures, which replaced trial by ordeal; the necessity of consent as the foundation of marriage; the need to show wrongful intent for conviction of crime, and legal protection of the poor against the rich.

The legacy of medieval "Christendom" had its darker side as well. From Christmas Day in 800, when Pope Leo III crowned Charlemagne as "Holy Roman Emperor," politics and religion were seldom separate. The results were mixed at best. Had the secular powers not defended Christianity, Europe might well be Muslim today. But the medieval Crusades to rescue the Holy Land from the Turks became excuses for plunder by conscripted thugs. Once church and state were yoked, almost any military action could be justified.

Although the New Testament contains no outline for a Christian society, medieval Christianity was one long effort to establish one. The doctrine the church preached became the doctrine the king enforced. Even Augustine had reluctantly concluded that the secular arm of society could be used to crush heresy. Acting on the premise that error has no rights, the church created the Inquisition, dispatching traveling squads of Franciscans and Dominicans to ferret out heretics. In 1252 Pope Innocent IV allowed suspects to be tortured. The guilty were imprisoned and sometimes put to death. Two centuries later, the Spanish monarchs Ferdinand and Isabella created a separate Inquisition aimed at discovering and expelling converted Jews and Muslims who secretly practiced their own religion. Even old women and children were tortured, and their descendants barred from universities and public office. In subsequent centuries Inquisitors expanded their list of heretics to include suspected Protestants and practitioners of witchcraft. Altogether, the Inquisition remains a monument to religious intolerance and a reminder of what can happen when church and state share total authority.

The Impact of Missionaries

The Reformation shattered the old Christendom but also unleashed new energies. Protestants translated the Bible into vernacular languages and encouraged lay learning and initiative. From Europe, Christian missionaries dispersed to Asia, Africa and the Americas. In many cases, it was a matter of the cross following the flag—a shameless blessing of imperialism and colonialism. But there are other ways of measuring the missionaries' impact. From the 16th-century Jesuits to the 19th-century Protestants, missionaries developed written languages for many "indigenous" peoples who had none—not to mention grammars and dictionaries. In this way, Protestant and Catholic missionaries "preserved local cultures that otherwise would have been swept away by global forces," says Mark Noll, professor of history at Wheaton College. The missionaries also established countless schools and hospitals, bringing literacy and modern medicine to those that the indigenous elites ignored. "Nelson Mandela," notes Noll, "is a graduate of two missionary schools."

As the world moves toward the third millennium,

Christianity seems far removed from the Jesus movement of its birth. And yet, the same gospel is being preached. Christians are still being persecuted: in the 20th century alone, there were many times more martyrs—especially under Hitler and Stalin—than all the victims of the Caesars combined. But the differences from times past are also striking. Post-Christian Europe seems spiritually exhausted. In the United States, secularism is the reigning ideology. However, there is more unity among Christians now than at any time since the Reformation. Despite the Holocaust—or perhaps because of it—"the people to whom Jesus belonged, and the people who belong to Jesus," as Pelikan puts it, are no longer spiritual enemies. Science and religion, once thought to be implacable adversaries, are beginning to talk to each other: the hubris of the Enlightenment has run its course.

Numerically, it is already clear, the future of Christianity lies with the youthful churches of Africa, the Hispanics of the Americas and—who knows?—the millions of stalwart Christians in China. Christianity already comprises the most diverse society known to humankind. But what new ideas and forms the gospel will inspire await the birth of the third millennium. Of the future, the Book of Revelation has only this to say: "Behold, I make all things new."

Current Trends in Christianity

by Philip Jenkins

Philip Jenkins, professor at Pennsylvania State University
in the Department of History and Religious Studies, is the
author of *The Next Christendom*, in which he explores current trends in Christianity and their possible outcomes.
He believes most of the Western world fails to understand the sweeping changes that are occurring in Christianity, which bear out the adage "History repeats itself."
Just as in the Reformation, Jenkins argues, Christianity is
being transformed by reformers targeting the corruption,
financial mismanagement, and abuses of power in the
church. Just as significant, Jenkins maintains, is the developing split between a more liberal Christianity in the
Northern Hemisphere and a neoconservative, orthodox
Christianity in the Southern Hemisphere.

The first Reformation was an epochal moment in the
history of the Western world—and eventually, by exten-
sion, of the rest of the world. The status quo in religious
affairs was brought to an end. Relations between religions and governments, not to mention among different denominations, took a variety of forms—sometimes
symbiotic, often chaotic and violent. The transforma-

tions wrought in the human psyche by the Reformation, and by the Counter-Reformation it helped to provoke, continue to play themselves out. This complex historical episode, which is now often referred to simply as "the Reformation," touched everything. It altered not just the practice of religion but also the nature of society, economics, politics, education, and the law.

How Christianity Will Influence the World

The fact is, we are at a moment as epochal as the Reformation itself—a Reformation moment not only for Catholics but for the entire Christian world. Christianity as a whole is both growing and mutating in ways that observers in the West tend not to see. For obvious reasons, news reports today are filled with material about the influence of a resurgent and sometimes angry Islam. But in its variety and vitality, in its global reach, in its association with the world's fastest-growing societies, in its shifting centers of gravity, in the way its values and practices vary from place to place—in these and other ways it is Christianity that will leave the deepest mark on the twenty-first century. The process will not necessarily be a peaceful one, and only the foolish would venture anything beyond the broadest predictions about the religious picture a century or two ahead. But the twenty-first century will almost certainly be regarded by future historians as a century in which religion replaced ideology as the prime animating and destructive force in human affairs, guiding attitudes to political liberty and obligation, concepts of nationhood, and, of course, conflicts and wars.

The original Reformation was far more than the rising up of irate lay people against corrupt and exploitative priests, and it was much more than a mere theological row. It was a far-reaching social movement that sought to return to the original sources of Christianity. It challenged the idea that divine authority should be mediated through institutions or hierarchies, and it denied the value of tradition. Instead it offered radical new notions of the supremacy of written texts (that is, the books of the Bible), interpreted by individual consciences. The Reformation made possible a religion that could be practiced privately, rather than mainly in a vast institutionalized community.

This move toward individualism, toward the privatization of religious belief, makes the spirit of the Reformation very attractive to educated people in the West. It stirs many liberal Catholic activists, who regard the aloof and arrogant hierarchy of the Church as not only an affront but something inherently corrupt. New concepts of governance sound exciting, even intoxicating, to reformers, and seem to mesh with likely social and technological trends. The invention of movable type and the printing press, in the fifteenth century, was a technological development that spurred mass literacy in the vernacular languages—and accelerated the forces of religious change. In the near future, many believe, the electronic media will have a comparably powerful impact on our ways of being religious.

A Christian Revolution

If we look beyond the liberal West, we see that another Christian revolution, quite different from the one being called for in affluent American suburbs and upscale urban parishes, is already in progress. Worldwide, Christianity is actually moving toward supernaturalism and neo-orthodoxy, and in many ways toward the ancient world view expressed in the New Testament: a vision of Jesus as the embodiment of divine power, who overcomes the evil forces that inflict calamity and sickness upon the human race. In the global South (the areas that we often think of primarily as the Third World) huge and growing Christian populations—currently 480 million in Latin America, 360 million in Africa, and 313 million in Asia, compared with 260 million in North America—now make up what the Catholic scholar Walbert Buhlmann has called the Third Church, a form of Christianity as distinct as Protestantism or Orthodoxy, and one that is likely to become dominant in the faith. The revolution taking place in Africa, Asia, and Latin America is far more sweeping in its implications than any current shifts in North American religion, whether Catholic or Protestant. There is increasing tension between what one might call a liberal Northern Reformation and the surging Southern religious revolution, which one might equate with the Counter-Reformation, the internal Catholic reforms that took place at the same time as the Reformation. No matter what the terminology, however, an enormous rift seems inevitable.

Although Northern governments are still struggling to come to terms with the notion that Islam might provide a powerful and threatening supranational ideology, few seem to realize the potential political role of ascendant Southern Christianity. . . .

Christian Population Shifts

The changes that Catholic and other reformers today are trying to inspire in North America and Europe (and that seem essential if Christianity is to be preserved as a modern, relevant force on those continents) run utterly contrary to the dominant cultural movements in the rest of the Christian world, which look very much like the Counter-Reformation. But this century is unlike the sixteenth in that we are not facing a roughly equal division of Christendom between two competing groups. Rather, Christians are facing a shrinking population in the liberal West and a growing majority of the traditional Rest. During the past half century the critical centers of the Christian world have moved decisively to Africa, to Latin America, and to Asia. The balance will never shift back.

The growth in Africa has been relentless. In 1900 Africa had just 10 million Christians out of a continental population of 107 million—about nine percent. Today the Christian total stands at 360 million out of 784 million, or 46 percent. And that percentage is likely to continue rising, because Christian African countries have some of the world's most dramatic rates of population growth. Meanwhile, the advanced industrial countries are experiencing a dramatic birth dearth. Within the next twenty-five years the population of the world's Christians is expected to grow to 2.6 billion (making Christianity by far the world's largest faith). By 2025, 50 percent of the Christian population will be in Africa and Latin America, and another 17 percent will be in Asia. Those proportions will grow steadily. By about 2050 the United States will still have the largest single contingent of Christians, but all the other leading nations will be Southern: Mexico, Brazil, Nigeria, the Democratic Republic of the Congo, Ethiopia, and the Philippines. By then the proportion of non-Latino whites among the world's Christians will have fallen to perhaps one in five.

The population shift is even more marked in the specifically Catholic world, where Euro-Americans are already in the minority. Africa had about 16 million Catholics in the early 1950s; it has 120 million today, and is expected to have 228 million by 2025. The *World Christian Encyclopedia* suggests that by 2025 almost three quarters of all Catholics will be found in Africa, Asia, and Latin America. The likely map of twenty-first-century Catholicism represents an unmistakable legacy of the Counter-Reformation and its global missionary ventures.

These figures actually understate the Southern predominance within Catholicism, and within world Christianity more generally, because they fail to take account of Southern emigrants to Europe and North America. Even as this migration continues, established white communities in Europe are declining demographically, and their religious beliefs and practices are moving further away from traditional Christian roots. The result is that skins of other hues are increasingly evident in European churches; half of all London churchgoers are now black. African and West Indian churches in Britain are reaching out to whites, though members complain that their religion is often seen as "a black thing" rather than "a God thing."

In the United States a growing proportion of Roman Catholics are Latinos, who should represent a quarter of the nation by 2050 or so. Asian communities in the United States have sizable Catholic populations. Current trends suggest that the religious values of Catholics with a Southern ethnic and cultural heritage will long remain quite distinct from those of other U.S. populations. In terms of liturgy and worship Latino Catholics are strikingly different from Anglo believers, not least in maintaining a fervent devotion to the Virgin Mary and the saints.

European and Euro-American Catholics will within a few decades be a smaller and smaller fragment of a worldwide Church. Of the 18 million Catholic baptisms recorded in 1998, eight million took place in Central and South America, three million in Africa, and just under three million in Asia. (In other words, these three regions already account for more than three quarters of all Catholic baptisms.) The annual baptism total for the Philippines is higher than the totals for Italy, France, Spain, and Poland combined. The number of Filipino Catholics could grow to 90 million by 2025, and perhaps to 130 million by 2050.

Shifts on Theology

The demographic changes within Christianity have many implications for theology and religious practice, and for global society and politics. The most significant point is that in terms of both theology and moral teaching, Southern Christianity is more conservative than the Northern—especially the American—version. Northern reformers, even if otherwise sympathetic to the indigenous cultures of non-Northern peoples, obviously do not like this fact. The liberal Catholic writer James Carroll has complained that "world Christianity [is falling] increasingly under the sway of anti-intellectual fundamentalism." But the cultural pressures may be hard to resist.

The denominations that are triumphing across the global South—radical Protestant sects, either evangelical or Pentecostal, and Roman Catholicism of an orthodox kind—are stalwartly traditional or even reactionary by the standards of the economically advanced nations. The Catholic faith that is rising rapidly in Africa and Asia looks very much like a pre-Vatican II faith, being more traditional in its respect for the power of bishops and priests and in its preference for older devotions. African Catholicism in particular is far more comfortable with notions of authority and spiritual charisma than with newer ideas of consultation and democracy.

Meanwhile, a full-scale Reformation is taking place among Pentecostal Christians—whose ideas are shared by many Catholics. Pentecostal believers reject tradition and hierarchy, but they also rely on direct spiritual revelation to supplement or replace biblical authority. And it is Pentecostals who stand in the vanguard of the Southern Counter-Reformation. Though Pentecostalism emerged as a movement only at the start of the twentieth century, chiefly in North America, Pentecostals today are at least 400 million strong, and heavily concentrated in the global South. By 2040 or so there could be as many as a billion, at which point Pentecostal Christians alone will far outnumber the world's Buddhists and will enjoy rough numerical parity with the world's Hindus.

The booming Pentecostal churches of Africa, Asia, and Latin America are thoroughly committed to re-creating their version of an idealized early Christianity (often described as the restoration of "primitive" Christianity). The most successful Southern churches preach a deep personal faith, communal orthodoxy, mysticism, and puritanism, all founded on obedience to spiritual authority, from whatever source it is believed to stem. Pentecostals—and their Catholic counterparts—preach messages that may appear simplistically charismatic, visionary, and apocalyptic to a Northern liberal. For them prophecy is an everyday reality, and many independent denominations trace their foundation to direct prophetic authority. Scholars of religion customarily speak of these proliferating congregations simply as the "prophetic churches.". . .

As predominantly rural societies have become more urban over the past thirty or forty years, millions of migrants have been attracted to ever larger urban areas, which lack the resources and the infrastructure to meet the needs of these wanderers. Sometimes people travel to cities within the same nation, but often they find themselves in different countries and cultures, suffering a still greater sense of estrangement. In such settings religious communities emerge to provide health, welfare, and education.

This sort of alternative social system, which played an enormous role in the earliest days of Christianity, has been a potent means of winning mass support for the most committed religious groups and is likely to grow in importance as the gap between people's needs and government's capacities to fill them becomes wider. Looking at the success of Christianity in the Roman Empire, the historian Peter Brown has written, "The Christian community suddenly came to appeal to men who felt deserted. . . . Plainly, to be a Christian in 250 brought more protection from one's fellows than to be a civis Romanus." Being a member of an active Christian church today may well bring more tangible benefits than being a mere citizen of Nigeria or Peru.

The desperate public-health situation in the booming mega-cities of the South goes far toward explaining the emphasis of the new churches on healing mind and body. In Africa in the early twentieth century an explosion of Christian healing movements and new prophets coincided with a dreadful series of epidemics, and the religious upsurge of those years was in part a quest for bodily health. Today African churches stand or fall by their success in healing, and elaborate rituals have formed around healing practices (though church members disagree on whether believers should rely entirely on spiritual assistance). The same interest in spiritual healing is found in what were once the mission churches—bodies such as the Anglicans and the Lutherans. Nowhere in the global South do the various spiritual healers find serious competition from modern scientific medicine: it is simply beyond the reach of most of the poor.

Disease, exploitation, pollution, drink, drugs, and violence, taken together, can account for why people might easily accept that they are under siege from demonic forces, and that only divine intervention can save them. Even radical liberation theologians use apocalyptic language on occasion. When a Northerner asks, in effect, where the Southern churches are getting such ideas, the answer is not hard to find: they're getting them from the Bible. Southern Christians are reading the New Testament and taking it very seriously; in it they see the power of Jesus fundamentally expressed through his confrontations with demonic powers, particularly those causing sickness and insanity. "Go back and report to John what you hear and see," Jesus says in the Gospel according to Matthew (11: 4-5). "The blind receive sight, the lame walk, those who have leprosy are cured, the deaf hear, the dead are raised, and the good news is preached to the poor." For the past two hundred years Northern liberals have employed various nonliteral interpretations of these healing passages—perhaps Jesus had a good sense of the causes and treatment of psychosomatic ailments? But that is not, of course, how such scenes are understood within the Third Church. . . .

The Catholic Church

The changing demographic balance between North and South helps to explain the current shape of world Catholicism, including the fact that the Church has been headed by Pope John Paul II. In the papal election of 1978 the Polish candidate won the support of Latin American cardinals, who were not prepared to accept yet another Western European. In turn, John Paul has recognized the growing Southern presence in the Church. Last year [2001] he elevated forty-four new cardinals, of whom eleven were Latin American, two Indian, and three African. The next time a papal election takes place, fifty-seven of the 135 cardinals eligible to vote, or more than 40 percent, will be from Southern nations. Early this century they will constitute a majority.

It may be true that from the liberal Northern perspective, pressure for a Reformation-style solution to critical problems in the Church—the crisis in clerical celibacy, the shortage of priests, the sense that the laity's concerns are ignored—seems overwhelming. Poll after poll in the United States and Europe indicates significant distrust of clerical authority and support for greater lay participation and women's equality. The obvious question in the parishes of the developed world seems to be how long the aloof hierarchy can stave off the forces of history.

From Rome, however, the picture looks different, as do the "natural" directions that history is going to take.

The Roman church operates on a global scale and has done so for centuries. Long before the French and British governments had become aware of global politics—and well before their empires came into being—papal diplomats were thinking through their approaches to China, their policies in Peru, their views on African affairs, their stances on the issues facing Japan and Mexico. To adapt a popular activist slogan, the Catholic Church not only thinks globally, it acts globally. That approach is going to have weighty consequences. On present evidence, a Southern-dominated Catholic Church is likely to react traditionally to the issues that most concern American and European reformers: matters of theology and devotion, sexual ethics and gender roles, and, most fundamentally, issues of authority within the Church.

The cultural gap between Christians of the North and the South will increase rather than diminish in the coming decades, for reasons that recall Luther's time. During the early modern period Northern and Southern Europe were divided between the Protestantism of the word and the Catholicism of the senses—between a religious culture of preaching, hymns, and Bible reading, and one of statues, rituals, and processions. Today we might see as a parallel the impact of electronic technologies, which is being felt at very different rates in the Northern and Southern worlds. The new-media revolution is occurring in Europe, North America, and the Pacific Rim while other parts of the globe are focusing on—indeed, still catching up with—the traditional world of book learning. Northern communities will move to ever more decentralized and privatized forms of faith as Southerners maintain older ideals of community and traditional authority.

Moral Concerns

On moral issues, too, Southern churches are far out of step with liberal Northern churches. African and Latin American churches tend to be very conservative on issues such as homosexuality and abortion. Such disagreement can pose real political difficulties for churches that aspire to a global identity and that try to balance diverse opinions. At present this is scarcely an issue for the Roman Catholic Church, which at least officially preaches the same conservatism for all regions. If, however, Church officials in North America or Europe proclaimed a moral stance more in keeping with progressive secular values, they would be divided from the growing Catholic churches of the South by a de facto schism, if not a formal breach.

The experience of the world's Anglicans and Episcopalians may foretell the direction of conflicts within the Roman Catholic Church. In the Anglican Communion, which is also torn by a global cultural conflict over issues of gender and sexuality, orthodox Southerners seek to re-evangelize a Euro-American world that they view as coming close to open heresy. This uncannily recalls the situation in sixteenth-century Europe, in which Counter-Reformation Catholics sent Jesuits and missionary priests to reconvert those regions that had fallen into Protestantism.

Anglicans in the North tend to be very liberal on homosexuality and the ordination of women. In recent years, however, liberal clerics have been appalled to find themselves outnumbered and regularly outvoted. In these votes the bishops of Africa and Asia have emerged as a rock-solid conservative bloc. The most ferocious battle to date occurred at the Lambeth World Conference in 1998, which adopted, over the objections of the liberal bishops, a forthright traditional statement proclaiming the impossibility of reconciling homosexual conduct with Christian ministry. As in the Roman Catholic Church, the predominance of Southerners at future events of this kind will only increase. Nigeria already has more practicing Anglicans than any other country, far more than Britain itself, and Uganda is not far behind. By mid-century the global total of Anglicans could approach 150 million, of whom only a small minority will be white Europeans or North Americans. The shifting balance within the church could become a critical issue very shortly, since the new Archbishop of Canterbury, Rowan Williams, is notably gay-friendly and has already ordained a practicing homosexual as a priest. . . .

Across the global South cardinals and bishops have become national moral leaders in a way essentially unseen in the West since the seventeenth century. The struggles of South African churches under apartheid spring to mind, but just as impressive were the pro-democracy campaigns of many churches and denominations elsewhere in Africa during the 1980s and 1990s. Prelates know that they are expected to speak for their people, even though if they speak boldly, they may well pay with their lives. Important and widely revered modern martyrs include Archbishop Luwum, of Uganda; Archbishop Munzihirwa, of Zaire; and Cardinal Biayenda, of Congo-Brazzaville.

Christianity and Politics

As this sense of moral leadership grows, we might reasonably ask whether Christianity will also provide a guiding political ideology for much of the world. We might even imagine a new wave of Christian states, in which political life is inextricably bound up with religious belief. Zambia declared itself a Christian nation in 1991, and similar ideas have been bruited in Zimbabwe, Kenya, and Liberia. If this ideal does gain popularity, the Christian South will soon be dealing with some debates, of long standing in the North, over the proper relationship between Church and State and between rival churches under the law. Other inevitable questions involve tolerance and diversity, the relationship between majority and minority communities, and the extent to which religiously inspired laws can (or should) regulate private morality and behavior. These issues were all at the core of the Reformation.

Across the regions of the world that will be the most populous in the twenty-first century, vast religious contests are already in progress, though so far they have impinged little on Western opinion. The most significant conflict is in Nigeria, a nation that by rights should be a major regional power in this century and perhaps even a global power; but recent violence between Muslims and Christians raises the danger that Nigerian society might be brought to ruin by the clash of jihad and crusade. Muslims and Christians are at each other's throats in Indonesia, the Philippines, Sudan, and a growing number of other African nations; Hindu extremists persecute Christians in India. Demographic projections suggest that these feuds will simply worsen. . . .

Perhaps the most remarkable point about these potential conflicts is that the trends pointing toward them have registered so little on the consciousness of even well-informed Northern observers. What, after all, do most Americans know about the distribution of

Christians worldwide? I suspect that most see Christianity very much as it was a century ago—a predominantly European and North American faith. In discussions of the recent sexual-abuse crisis "the Catholic Church" and "the American Church" have been used more or less synonymously.

As the media have striven in recent years to present Islam in a more sympathetic light, they have tended to suggest that Islam, not Christianity, is the rising faith of Africa and Asia, the authentic or default religion of the world's huddled masses. But Christianity is not only surviving in the global South, it is enjoying a radical revival, a return to scriptural roots. We are living in revolutionary times.

But we aren't participating in them. By any reasonable assessment of numbers, the most significant transformation of Christianity in the world today is not the liberal Reformation that is so much desired in the North. It is the Counter-Reformation coming from the global South. And it's very likely that in a decade or two neither component of global Christianity will recognize its counterpart as fully or authentically Christian.

Glossary

agnostic: A person who does not believe there is proof for the existence of God but admits that there is a possibility that God exists.

Albigenses: Members of a Catholic religious group condemned for heresy in the twelfth and thirteenth centuries.

anchorite: A person who has retired to solitude for religious reasons.

Anglican: Relating to the Church of England.

anti-Semitic: Showing hostility toward the Jews.

apocalyptic: Having to do with doom or disaster.

apocryphal: Of questionable authority or authenticity.

apologetic: A formal defense of the Christian faith.

Arianism: The doctrine of Arius, who taught that Jesus was not the same substance as God the Father.

canon: Books of the Bible officially accepted as authentic.

Catholic: The universal, undivided church.

celibacy: Abstaining from marriage and sexual relations.

cloister: Another name for a monastery.

Communion: The ceremony that involves partaking in bread and wine, representing the body and blood of Jesus.

conversion: Changing to a new faith.

Counter-Reformation: Reform that took place within the Catholic Church in response to the Protestant Reformation.

creed: A formal, brief statement of the key elements of one's faith.

ecclesiastical: Relating to the church.

ecumenical: Relating to unity among all religions.

election: A Christian belief that God selected people for salvation.

encyclical: A papal letter addressed to members of the church.

episcopal: Relating to bishops.

Episcopalian: Belonging to the Episcopal Church (closely related to the Church of England).

evangelicals: Protestants who believe in the authority of the Bible and personal salvation in the name of Jesus for eternal life.

evangelism: Spreading the gospel of Jesus with enthusiasm.

fundamentalism: An organized, determined branch of Protestantism that opposes liberal church theology.

gentile: A person who is not a Jew.

grace: Unmerited favor of God.

heretic: Someone who holds opinions that are not accepted by traditional Christians.

homily: A sermon based on passages from the Bible.

humanism: A system of thought that focuses on people rather than God.

icon: An image.

incarnation: Jesus as God coming into the world as a human.

indulgence: A remission of punishment for sin.

laity: The nonordained members of a church.

lay preacher: Someone who preaches without formal training in a divinity school.

liturgy: The form of public worship adopted by a church.

Lord's Supper: Same as the Last Supper; Communion.

Messiah: The Jewish savior who would deliver his people.

neoorthodoxy: A Protestant movement that opposed liberal theology.

nihilism: A doctrine that says nothing can be known and all is without value.

ordinances: Christian laws and regulations.

ordination: Official appointment of someone to the ministry.

pagan: A heathen, non-Christian.

pantheism: A belief that God is the universe; a toleration of all gods.

parish: A small, administrative section of some church organizations; a local church community.

Passover: A Jewish holiday that commemorates when God delivered the Israelites from Egyptian slavery.

patriarch: Title of a high-ranking bishop in some churches.

penitent: A person who performs penance for sins.

Pentecostal: Having to do with churches that emphasize the action of the Holy Spirit.

Platonic: Having to do with the teachings of Plato, who stressed transcendental values of an ideal world.

polemic: An argument involving controversial matters.

predestination: The belief that God selected who should be saved.

proselytes: Newly converted people.

Providence: The care of God in human affairs.

Psalter: A book of Psalms from the Bible; sometimes set to music.

Puritan: A member of a Protestant group in England during the sixteenth and seventeenth centuries that wanted simplified church ceremonies.

Reformation: The sixteenth-century break with Catholicism that resulted in Protestant churches.

revival: A meeting held to stir people to greater religious fervor.

sacerdotal: Having to do with priests.

sacrament: A rite conducted by a church.

Savior: A term for Jesus signifying one who saves another from harm.

schism: A breaking up into smaller factions.

scholasticism: The chief philosophy of the Middle Ages based on Aristotle and the church fathers.

secular: Of the world rather than of the religious spirit.

Septuagint: A Greek translation of the Hebrew Bible created in the third century before Jesus.

Stoicism: A philosophy that urges people to be free from passion.

synagogue: A place for Jews to worship God.

synod: A council of church leaders.

Trinity: The Christian doctrine that says there is one God with three personalities (the Father, the Son, and the Holy Spirit).

Waldenses: A Christian group that accepted the doctrines of John Calvin, a Protestant reformer.

Chronology

30
Jesus is crucified and resurrected; the church starts at Pentecost.

35
Paul converts to Christianity.

46
Paul begins missionary journeys.

47
The Council of Jerusalem frees Gentile believers from Jewish law.

57
Paul writes his letter to the Romans.

64
The fire of Rome occurs; the emperor Nero blames Christians and launches persecutions of them.

70
Titus and his Roman army destroy Jerusalem.

312
Constantine converts to Christianity.

313

The Edict of Milan changes Christianity from a persecuted sect to a tolerated religion.

325

The Council of Nicea approves the idea that Jesus is fully God.

386

Augustine converts to Christianity.

405

Jerome completes the Vulgate, his Latin translation of the Bible.

432

Patrick begins his mission to convert the Irish.

540

Benedict writes his rule that makes monasticism practical.

988

Russia converts to the Eastern Orthodox faith.

1054

The Great Schism occurs, in which the eastern and western churches split.

1095

The First Crusade is launched.

1272

Thomas Aquinas finishes his *Summa Theologiae*.

1453
Constantinople falls to Islam, marking the end of the Eastern Roman Empire.

1456
Johannes Gutenberg produces the first printed Bible.

1517
Martin Luther posts his Ninety-five Theses.

1525
The Anabaptist movement starts, making the Reformation more radical.

1534
England breaks away from the Catholic Church and creates the Anglican Church.

1536
John Calvin writes the first edition of his *Institutes of the Christian Religion.*

1540
Ignatius of Loyola gains approval for the Society of Jesus (the Jesuits).

1563
John Foxe's *Book of Martyrs* is published.

1611
The King James Version of the Bible is published.

1647
George Fox, founder of the Quakers, begins to preach.

1735
George Whitefield, a preacher associated with the Great Awakening, converts to Christianity.

1738
John and Charles Wesley are converted to evangelical Christianity.

1740
The Great Awakening reaches its peak.

1793
William Carey leaves as a missionary to India.

1807
William Wilberforce, an English Christian, leads the abolition of the slave trade.

1844
The first Adventist churches are formed.

1865
J. Hudson Taylor founds the China Inland Mission.

1870
The First Vatican Council declares papal infallibility.

1878
William and Catherine Booth found the Salvation Army.

1906
A revival meeting led by William J. Seymour launches Pentecostalism.

1931

C.S. Lewis becomes a Christian.

1934

Wycliffe Bible Translators is founded.

1942

The National Association of Evangelicals begins.

1948

The World Council of Churches is organized.

1949

An evangelical crusade in Los Angeles creates fame for Billy Graham.

1950

Missionaries are forced to leave China due to a Communist takeover. Mother Teresa founds Missionaries of Charity to help the poor and sick.

1962

The Second Vatican Council opens.

1963

Reverend Martin Luther King Jr. leads the March on Washington to protest racism.

1974

The Lausanne Congress on World Evangelization is held.

1979

Pope John Paul II visits Poland for the first time since his elevation to the papacy.

For Further Research

Books

Roland Bainton, *Christendom*. 2 vols. New York: Harper & Row, 1964.

Benson Bobrick, *Wide as the Waters: The Story of the English Bible and the Revolution It Inspired*. New York: Penguin, 2001.

Martin Brecht, *Martin Luther*. 2 vols. Philadelphia: Fortress, 1985, 1994.

Peter Brown, *The Rise of Western Christendom*. Cambridge, MA: Blackwell, 1996.

Thomas Cahill, *Desire of the Everlasting Hills: The World Before and After Jesus*. New York: Anchor, 2001.

———, *How the Irish Saved Civilization*. New York: Anchor, 1995.

Earle Edwin Cairns, *Christianity Through the Centuries: A History of the Christian Church*. Grand Rapids, MI: Academie, 1981.

Vincent Carroll and David Shiflett, *Christianity on Trial*. San Francisco: Encounter, 2002.

Robert G. Clouse, Richard V. Pierard, and Edwin M. Yamauchi, *Two Kingdoms: The Church and Culture Through the Ages*. Chicago: Moody, 1993.

Tim Dowley, ed., *Eerdmans' Handbook to the History of Christianity*. Grand Rapids, MI: Eerdmans, 1977.

William A. Dyrness, *Emerging Voices in Global Theology.* Grand Rapids, MI: Zondervan, 1994.

Richard P. Heitzenrater, *Wesley and the People Called Methodists.* Nashville: Abingdon, 1995.

Paul Johnson, *A History of Christianity.* New York: Atheneum, 1976.

Martin D.W. Jones, ed., *The Counter Reformation: Religion and Society in Early Modern Europe.* New York: Cambridge University Press, 1995.

D. James Kennedy and Jerry Newcombe, *What If Jesus Had Never Been Born?* Nashville: Thomas Nelson, 1994.

Kenneth Scott Latourette, *A History of the Expansion of Christianity.* Grand Rapids, MI: Zondervan, 1970.

Carter Lindberg, *The European Reformations.* Cambridge, MA: Blackwell, 1996.

Charles Lippy, Robert Choquette, and Stafford Poole, *Christianity Comes to the Americas.* New York: Paragon House, 1992.

Clyde L. Manschreck, *A History of Christianity in the World.* Englewood Cliffs, NJ: Prentice-Hall, 1974.

David Martin, *Tongues of Fire: The Explosion of Protestantism in Latin America.* Oxford, UK: Blackwell, 1990.

Alister McGrath, *In the Beginning: The Story of the King James Bible.* New York: Random House, 2001.

Lynn Hartley Millar, *Christian Education in the First Four Centuries.* London: Faith Press, 1946.

Stephen Neill, *A History of Christian Missions.* New York: Penguin, 1964.

Richard John Neuhaus, ed., *The Second One Thousand Years: Ten People Who Defined a Millennium.* Grand Rapids, MI: Eerdmans, 2001.

Mark A. Noll, *The Scandal of the Evangelical Mind.* Grand Rapids, MI: Eerdmans, 1994.

————, *Turning Points: Decisive Moments in the History of Christianity.* Grand Rapids, MI: Baker Academic, 2000.

Lars Qualben, *A History of the Christian Church.* New York: Thomas Nelson and Sons, 1958.

M.A. Smith, *From Christ to Constantine.* Downers Grove, IL: InterVarsity, 1971.

Gayla Visalli, *After Jesus.* Pleasantville, NY: Reader's Digest, 1992.

Williston Walker, *A History of the Christian Church.* New York: Scribner's, 1985.

Andrew F. Walls, *The Missionary Movement in Christian History.* Maryknoll, NY: Orbis, 1996.

Timothy Ware, *The Orthodox Church.* New York: Penguin, 1993.

Web Sites

Australian Catholic University, www.mcauley.acu.edu.au/~yuri /ecc. This site provides a Catholic perspective on church history. It includes a detailed bibliography for further reading.

Bible History Online, www.bible-history.com. Even though this is a Christian site, it has many links to non-Christian sites for further information. The topics covered include church fathers, creeds, heresies, timelines, and key individuals.

Christianbook, www.christianbook.com. A huge number of books for sale are listed here for further study, including best-sellers, works by key historians, and original works by writers and theologians.

Interactive Bible, www.bible.ca/history. This site contains information on church history and the writings of many church fathers.

North Park University, www.campus.northpark.edu/history/
WebChron/Christianity/Christianity.html. The school offers a chronology plus selected articles on various events:
the apostolic era, the early church, the church in Germanic Europe, the church in Eastern Europe, the church
outside of Europe, and world Christianity.

Ontario Consultants on Religious Tolerance, www.religious
tolerance.org/chr_ch.htm. Recent trends in Christianity
are covered here, as are interesting tidbits of Christian history such as the Shroud of Turin and the bone box of
James. There is also information on the early years of
Christian history to A.D. 600.

Scroll Publishing, www.scrollpublishing.com. In addition to
offering information on books for sale, the site discusses
key persons, places, and movements associated with the
history of Christianity.

Wake Forest University, www.wfu.edu/~matthet1/perspectives
/index.html. The university has posted here lectures from
its class titled "Religion 166: Religious Life in the United
States." It covers everything from the Puritans to African
American religion.

Wikipedia, http://en.wikipedia.org/wiki/History_of_Christianity.
This free encyclopedia contains a great deal of information on the history of Christianity.

Yutopian Online, www.yutopian.com/religion. This site gives
information about Christianity in China: its history, historic
sites, missionaries, and Chinese Christians.

Index